Contents

About the author

Pepe Nummi has led international and virtual teams since 1990 and worked as a facilitator since 1998. Pepe is one of the founders of the company Grape People, which focuses on facilitation training and services for businesses around the world. On top of all of this, Pepe is one of the developers of Idealogue, and is the author of the Facilitator's handbook[1] and the Virtual Facilitators Handbook[2]. Over the course of his long career, he has provided facilitation services in over 20 countries, and has also trained over 10,000 facilitators. Pepe's extensive experience with facilitation makes this a very practical book for everyone working with groups.

---

[1] Published in Finnish, Russian and Chinese.
[2] Published in Finnish.

Pepe Nummi

BEYOND BRAINSTORMING
– Idealogue

© Grape People Finland Oy
Publisher Grape People Finland Oy

Layout: Oy Graaf Ab / Jani Osolanus

ISBN 978-952-93-7343-7

Helsinki, Finland 2016

Foreword

By Amanda Stott

The first time I heard about Idealogue was in Slovenia 2002, while attending The International Conference for Facilitators. I spent the afternoon with about thirty other facilitators who had also chosen to attend an afternoon workshop led by Pepe Nummi. It was there in that workshop that Pepe introduced us to something new and exciting; Idealogue. I was not disappointed and over the past 14 years I have used ideologue to support many groups during facilitated sessions and introduced hundreds and hundreds of trainee facilitators to the method and encouraged them to steal it with pride!

The beauty of the method is in its simplicity. As Pepe takes the reader around the world in his stories about working with his clients in Africa, China, and closer to home in Scandinavia, he demonstrates the application of Idealogue in many phases of the problem solving and change cycle, and he provides insight into how to use the method with groups of different sizes.

Beyond Brainstorming – Idealogue will allow both novice and seasoned facilitators to reflect on what is required and what happens when the group they are working with needs to identify and prioritize issues, ideas, options or actions. To me, the beauty of the process is that Idealogue is structured so that it invokes the use of Roger Shwarz's Ground Rules for Effective Groups in opening conversation about the ideas that people first generate and share; more specifically 'explain your reasoning and intent ', 'test assumptions and inferences', and 'combine advocacy with inquiry'. As these ground rules are followed, groups move gradually through Sam Kaner's 'Groan Zone', shifting from individual divergence of ideas towards group convergence by sharing their values, reasoning, and experience all while building commitment along the way.

In addition to just presenting Idealogue in this book, I am happy to say that Pepe's playfulness and personality also shine through in this text as he shares stories of using the tool, enriched with the context, the characters and the discourse shaping the flow and progress through each session. Pepe offers so much more than Idealogue in the book; by sharing his thinking ahead of working with groups he offers insight into how to plan and prepare for facilitating a session; in sharing his interactions within the groups he demonstrates interventions to support group effectiveness, and in sharing his sample workshop structures, he provides the reader with ideas to engage, stimulate and embed.

Since 2002 I have used "steal with pride" with great Pride, and I have seen firsthand how it enables people to listen to and understand other people's ideas. I hope you enjoy reading *Beyond Brainstorming – Idealogue*, and after doing so I hope you decide to steal with pride too!

Amanda Stott is a professional facilitator who holds a degree in Sports Science from Birmingham University, and a Master's degree in Behavioral Science from Leeds Polytechnic. In 1999 she founded facilitate this!, a company specializing in facilitation training and services.

Chapter 1

Introduction

Brainstorming methods are still widely used, and people use the word brainstorming when they think about the process of creating new ideas. Brainstorming is useful, as it should be, but current brainstorming practices are inadequate and give meager results. While it is true that traditional brainstorming methods help discover new ideas, they do not help people understand, internalize, or prioritize new ideas. Here is where Idealogue can help. Idealogue is a revolution against conventional brainstorming techniques, and it fills the gap left by the shortcomings of brainstorming methods. This book takes Idealogue into different types of meetings and workshops to show how it can be used with other facilitation tools to create dynamic meetings to help people problem solve and produce results.

Idealogue is the result of a series of attempts to use dialogue to help people connect during meetings, workshops, or brainstorming sessions. One reoccurring challenge during brainstorming sessions getting people to truly listen to one another. More often than not, individuals want to make sure that their own ideas are heard and understood and they have little time to focus on the ideas of others. This dynamic presents a real challenge of how to connect their ideas with the ideas of others and to form a common understanding.

Idealogue can be used in many different working contexts. This book begins with an introduction to Idealogue and the theory behind it. In the following chapters, Idealogue will be shown at work in different meeting types to achieve a variety of objectives; problem solving, visioning, creativity, change deployment, and action planning. Chapters open with practical stories on how to use Idealogue in the real world and the stories explain how Idealogue works in these different situations. Idealogue is most effective when paired with other communication and facilitative tools, and examples of creating a sound workshop or meeting structure by combining Idealogue with other tools will presented and explained.

The book concludes with the chapter titled, "Planning a Workshop." This chapter shows how the different types of goals or meeting types discussed in earlier chapters can be used in combination for a one day or a multi-day workshop.

Now let's begin with a short explanation of what decision making is and why Idealogue is more effective than traditional brainstorming methods.

What is a Decision?

I enjoy ice cream. In fact, I eat ice cream every Sunday for breakfast. I love this routine so much that I wake my two kids up early so they can eat ice-cream with me. I know that this habit is unusual for most people but I have my reasons for it and it makes sense to me. This is a decision I have made but it is not a self-contained decision. My entire belief system is connected to the fact that I eat ice cream on Sundays. First and foremost, there is the belief that I love ice-cream. This could be the most prominent belief.

Secondly, my kids love ice-cream and I believe that they like the idea of me waking them up early Sunday morning for ice cream because it is feels special to them. I also believe that my wife hates this practice of giving the kids ice cream for breakfast. This belief is confirmed by the dirty looks I get when serving it to them. I have a strong feeling that she would be furious if I did this on a regular basis, but I am quite sure that everything is fine as long as the ice cream breakfasts are limited to just Sundays.

There is another belief relating to this habit which is that I have more time to enjoy eating ice -cream on Sundays. Actually, I have time to eat ice-cream several times a day but somehow eating ice-cream in a hurry just does not seem right to me. And finally, I believe that ice-cream makes me fat. Therefore, I choose to eat ice-cream just once a week to limit its consumption, and to maintain my athletic figure. If we would explore this belief of limiting my portions of ice-cream, we would hit an entire new belief system consisting of many ideas related to who I am, what I eat, how I want to appear, and what health means to me.

In Summary, my beliefs are:

- I like ice-cream.
- My kids love ice-cream.
- My kids love being woken on Sunday mornings for ice-cream.
- My wife may not like the idea of me giving ice cream to our kids for breakfast on a regular basis.
- I have more time to enjoy eating ice-cream on Sundays.
- Ice-cream makes me fat.

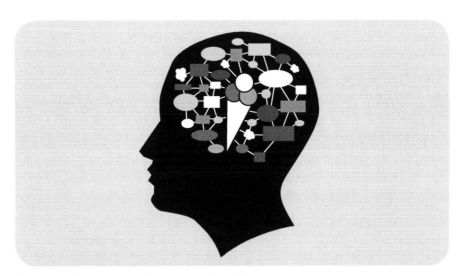

Figure 1: Decisions are embedded in our belief system.

Taking into consideration all of these beliefs, I decided to eat ice cream only on Sunday mornings for breakfast. I have made this decision because it is the most logical conclusion that connects all my aforementioned beliefs and assumptions. This is what decision-making feels like. A decision may sound or appear silly to other people when it is isolated and looked at without context. But to the decision maker, it is completely logical because the decision is in line with a larger belief system.

How does this affect group decision making? Imagine being part of a travelling group of students that holds a traditional brainstorming session every morning to decide what to eat at breakfast. Everyone gives different food choices like bread, cereal, pancakes, bacon, or omelets. No-one was allowed to criticize the ideas of others, and after the suggestions are given the group prioritizes them and decides to have bacon and cereal for breakfast. Unfortunately this decision is not a good one because two members of the group are allergic to cereal and another three are vegan.

Traditional brainstorming methods do not work because they do not create understanding of the ideas and the beliefs behind the ideas. The rules of classical brainstorming call for no criticism of the ideas produced, and without criticism it is difficult to understand someone else's ideas. In order to reach a sound decision, we need to first understand the underlying beliefs, values and facts that are behind the ideas and opinions of others. Idealogue actively encourages people to seek out, listen to, question and discover the assumptions and the logic that lies behind people's thoughts and ideas, helping to discover shared interests and support convergence towards group consensus. This book will demonstrate Idealogue in action.

Rules of classical brainstorming:

1. Withhold criticism
2. Go for quantity instead of quality
3. Welcome unusual ideas
4. Build on and expand the ideas of others

The key challenge of classical brainstorming:
You cannot critisize! If you do not ask why an idea makes sense or why it is valid, there is no deep understanding of the idea or the beliefs behind the idea.

Figure 2: Rules of classical brainstorming and the key challenge.

Chapter 2

Welcome to the World of Facilitation

Idealogue is a facilitation tool at heart, and I can't write about Idealogue without first defining what facilitation is, what the core elements of facilitation are, and what facilitation hopes to achieve. If you already are familiar with facilitation then you can skip this short section.

The Challenge

In offices around the world people are not connecting. Ideas are lost or left unsaid, and strategies are not understood. This is not by choice, nor due to a lack of effort. A lot of the time people cannot connect because workshops or meetings are improperly structured, with too many things happening at once.

Every meeting is driven by two core elements; content and process. Content refers to what people talk about in a meeting; the ideas, suggestions, and decisions that come up in group discussions. Process refers to how people communicate, make decisions, and solve problems as a group. What order are topics presented? Who speaks and for how long? How is feedback received and given? These are all aspects relating to the process of a meeting.

Unfortunately for us, the brain is not equipped to handle both content and process simultaneously. We are too preoccupied with the content, which makes the process suffer. People tend to focus on their own needs and ideas and on the topics that pertain the most to their own work. This makes it almost impossible to be receptive to or understand new, unfamiliar ideas. People are participating in the same conversation, but everyone is discussing a different aspect of the topic: one participant talks about facts, another one about solutions, someone else about the problem, a fourth person about their own feelings respective to the problem, and a final person about the weather. And the more people there are participating in a session, the more difficult it gets. This is the challenge that makes facilitation relevant.

The Solution

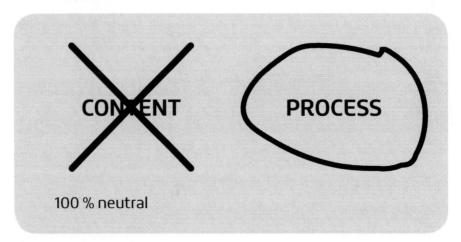

Figure 3: The role of a facilitator.

A facilitator is a neutral party that coordinates group meetings and workshops. Facilitators are neutral in the sense that they do not contribute to the content of the meeting or workshop in any way. They do not have a stake in the outcome including which decisions are prioritized during the meeting. They focus solely on the process of the meeting.

Therefore, the group provides the content of the meeting while the facilitator handles the process. By focusing on the process, the facilitator is able to help the group connect with one another to achieve better results.

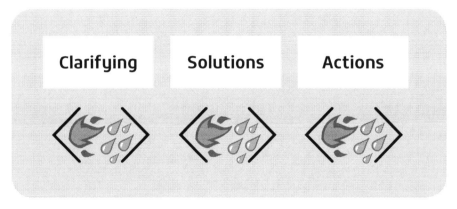

Figure 4: Stages of a workshop.

The process of facilitation consists of two key elements; stages and tools. Instead of allowing everyone in a meeting to talk freely about whatever they want whenever they want, the facilitator breaks a workshop into specific stages to keep the group on the same page. The typical stages of a workshop start with a *clarifying* stage, followed by a *solutions* stage and finally an *action* stage. These stages create a solid structure that tools can be added to, ultimately resulting in a group that is working together, in harmony. The stages will be explained in depth in Chapter 9: Planning a Workshop.

The second element of facilitation is the tools. The stages are nice in theory, but if the correct tools are not used, then the structure of a workshop falls flat. For each stage the facilitator needs to select the right set of tools to help the group create and choose their best ideas.

In short, there are three elements that make a significant contribution to the quality of a meeting or workshop; a facilitator that focuses on the process of the meeting instead of the content, simple stages that keep people on the same page, and tools that help people participate and make decisions.

The Value

Engaging the workforce by using facilitation leads to better understanding, the use of everyone's potential, organizational development, group alignment, and true commitment to strategic plans and company vision. These benefits may seem like ambitious promises, but when communication is improved and facilitation is used, people feel that they are contributing to decision making and that their voices are being heard. All of this contributes to greater understanding, increased employee happiness, and more company success!

Figure 5: Facilitation creates understanding and alignment.

The basic principle of facilitation is clear and simple; a neutral party focused solely on the process of a meeting can improve communication at the group level, and give people a sense of ownership over the decisions and ideas produced.

However, helping people communicate, connect, and truly understand each other's ideas can still be challenging even when using a neutral facilitator. Thankfully, Idealogue shines at addressing this challenge.

Chapter 3

Idealogue – the Method

Psssst! I have a confession to make. Idealogue is not something I dreamt up in a moment of divine inspiration. Nor is it something I spent years perfecting in a dusty library through academic study. It actually emerged through work experience and I am extremely proud of it. The amount of times I personally have used Idealogue number in the thousands, and fortunately I fortunate to have colleagues who commonly utilize Idealogue too. Developing and fine tuning Idealogue was not all champagne and self-congratulation. The process actually began with a series of failures and lessons.

The First Failure

It was springtime, in 2002 and a large North-European print house was at a crossroads. They didn't know what to do with Barbara. Who you ask? Big Barbara, their huge old printing machine. Due to her advanced age, Big Barbara used an absurd amount of energy to operate and she just couldn't keep up with the pace of modern business. Therefore, the company ordered a smaller, faster, and more flexible machine. Despite her place in history and in the hearts of employees, Big Barbara was about to become unemployed.

I was asked to facilitate a creativity session with the goal to find new uses for the legendary and beloved Big Barbara. The turnout for the session was great, with many different departments well represented. Everyone was well prepared for the session, which took place in the amazing 18th century island fortress of Suomenlinna, located in the Baltic Sea just off of the city of Helsinki. Everyone was comfortably situated in a brewery on the island with their favorite drinks in hand, ready to help decide the fate of Big Barbara.

Hundreds of ideas were generated using different brainstorming methods. Everyone was eager to share their thoughts on the best way to send Barbara off to retirement, and the walls of the brewery were soon covered in colorful papers, each with an idea written on it.

The best ideas were described, selected, further developed, and finally evaluated by all participants. When we closed the session everyone *seemed* happy, but unfortunately, looks can be deceiving.

Mr. Virtanen[3], who at that time was the Director of the printing house, had some concerns he wanted to discuss with me.

"Pepe, I think the session started off well, and there was no shortage of creative, usable ideas. But something went wrong when ideas were selected. The ideas that were chosen by the group are mediocre at best. We decided on these ideas together, but I still don't understand all of them. I don't know what happened."

Mr. Virtanen was left confused after the session and he was not entirely happy with the ideas the group decided on.

Lesson 1
While the session succeeded in creating many ideas, it failed to generate good understanding of the ideas. I learned that before the group can begin selecting or prioritizing ideas, I should help the group create a better understanding of the ideas.

The Second Failure

Flash forward a few weeks. The scene for the second failure brings us to the same island fortress of Suomenlinna, but in a different restaurant and with a new group. I was facilitating a creativity training workshop for a team of developers who were working on building the next great App that they hoped would take over the world, or failing that, at least domestic markets. We were in the process of creating ideas. I had the lessons from the first failure firmly in my mind, and I was trying to consciously focus on creating a good understanding of all ideas.

I thought that the answer was sharing ideas by back and forth conversation. I thought the answer was dialogue. I had read everything that was available on

---

[3] Name changed at the polite request of my dear customers

the art of conversation and I was ready to take the group into deeper conversational waters. The goal of adding dialogue to the session was to force participants to listen to each other. I hoped that by promoting dialogue in the session, a clear understanding of the ideas and motivations of others would come through.

With these thoughts running through my head I addressed the group.

"OK everyone, you all have done a great job so far. You have created many ideas. Now it is time to expand on these by discussing them with each other. You will not just state your ideas and then wait for while others do the same, instead in your groups you will *dialogue* with one another. This will help everyone understand and learn from each other. "

I continued on by starting to explain the ground rules of dialogue. One of the ground rules instructed participants to slow down the speed of conversation by speaking clearly and repeating anything that needed clarification.

One of the developers, a man called Mike, took this rule quite literally.

"Heeeeeeeey, how sloooow do youuuuu expeeeect uus to speeaak?" he deliberately asked, as the rest of the group laughed.

What is Dialogue ?
- Dia and Logos (Greek) = through meaning
- Focused and intentional conversation.
- An exchange of ideas or opinions.

Ground Rules of Dialogue
- Listen to understand, even when you disagree
- Search for assumptions
- Others have the right to believe and feel differently than you
- Do not interrupt when others share
- Treat others with respect and as equals
- Slow down the speed of conversation
- Share your own views
- Try not to rush to judgment
- Look for common ground
- Keep dialogue and decision-making separate (dialogue comes first)

Figure 6: A definition of dialogue and its ground rules.

I broke the group down into smaller groups of four to five, and told everyone to get to work. The groups had twenty-five minutes for group discussion, with an emphasis on giving each and every person enough time to express their own ideas, and also to ask questions about what other people were thinking. In about five minutes Mike's group was ready. "Pepe, we have some good ideas and we want to develop them further with everyone else. We are done with this dialogue stuff."I couldn't believe that the group was ready and I told him that while I appreciated their enthusiasm to continue, I still thought that they could talk more in order to better understand each other's ideas.

Hardly five more minutes passed before another group started to complain.

"Pepe, we have slowed down the pace and everything but I think we have already covered everything." I knew that it was impossible to create understanding of multiple technical ideas and concepts in just ten minutes, but I gave up and brought everyone back together in one large group, where we continued to develop ideas until the session ended.

Lesson 2

I left this session a bit frustrated with the participants. People do not want to listen to each other! The challenge with this particular creativity session was that the participants were either not willing or not able to listen to others while they had their own ideas. Later on when working with other groups I learned that this was not an isolated problem that was unique to this particular creativity session, but a problem with people in general: we just do not want to listen to others when we feel that we have a good idea ourselves.

Success: Birth of Idealogue

While I was experiencing these failures during idea generation sessions, I had a very helpful mentor named Kari Helin, who is a guru on group facilitation methods. I thought he would be the perfect person to help me with this issue. I explained everything as I saw it from my perspective and he gave an interesting response. He suggested that the participants should copy ideas from each other.

"Just make sure everyone has a piece of paper and let them go around copying ideas," said Kari. It almost sounded like too simple of a solution, but I decided to give it a try.

I was back working with the print house for a second workshop as Big Barbara was still in danger of becoming unemployed. First, I asked the participants to write down their ideas concerning Big Barbara's next step and if she could be used for something else or be recycled in some way. Next, I simply instructed participants to 'copy' ideas from others and write down what they thought the best of them were. This inspired the participants to be more competitive, and this competitiveness forced them to become inquisitive about other people's ideas. At the end of the session when the best ideas were selected and posted, the chosen ideas were already understood by almost everyone. The 'copying' had been successful in creating a shared reality among the participants. We had found a way that helped group members connect their ideas with other ideas. Idealogue was taking form, but it still was a long way from being ready.

The invaluable and generous help given to me by my colleagues helped me finalize Idealogue. I attended a workshop facilitated by Per Kristianssen from Denmark and he was talking about stealing with pride. I thought that was a fantastic ground rule for copying other people's ideas. Later on I learned that the phrase Steal with Pride was widely used by many organizational developers to fight the "not invented here" behavior which was stopping people from learning from other organizations.

Figure 7: The original Idealogue logo was designed by Pekka Leskelä.

I had one colleague who participated in the first trials of the method and who contributed a great deal. His name is Dr. Greg O'Shea, and in his work with groups he too was looking to improve group level comprehension of new ideas. He actually was the one who came up with the name 'Idealogue', by combining the terms 'idea' and 'dialogue', making Idealogue a conversation or exchange of ideas. Pekka Leskelä also helped in a significant way, by designing the very first logo for Idealogue.

Together we experimented with different variations of the method and different group sizes. Finally I stepped in by putting everything together and describing the process and its steps. Idealogue was ready.

In the beginning we used Idealogue in creativity sessions only. Quickly we discovered that people generally had problems connecting with others and understanding each other's ideas in other contexts too, so we began to use Idealogue in other types of meetings. Now we use Idealogue regularly in all sorts of different contexts, as it creates a good connection and creates a shared reality among group members.

I first introduced Idealogue at the 2003 conference of the International Association of Facilitators, which was held in Slovenia. Later on, it was published in *The Facilitator's Handbook* which I wrote in 2007. I have used Idealogue myself hundreds, if not thousands of times to get people to understand and connect around the best ideas produced in group settings, and I am proud to say that many other facilitators have added this method to their own toolboxes.

Now you probably got the point. I stole Idealogue. Or maybe it just emerged and was a happy accident of sorts. Anyhow, I now teach it and use it with pride and joy.

> **Dialogue= *dia+logos(greek)=through meaning***
>
> **Idealogue=Idea+dialogue = conversation to discover through meaning of ideas**

Figure 8: The definition of Idealogue.

The Method

Idealogue is made up of five stages; *Individual Stage, Steal with Pride Stage, Repeated Stealing Stage, Ideas Selection Stage,* and *Ideas Evaluation* Stage, which I will describe in detail below. The order of the stages always stays the same, but the amount of time spent on each stage can change, depending on the size of the group and the complexity of the topics being discussed.

Stage 1: Individual Stage

To begin, participants are asked to write down their ideas in silence.

People have different styles of thinking or reasoning. The same can be said about how they express their thoughts. Some people need to spend some time thinking before speaking while others can do both almost simultaneously. Therefore, it is vital to consider these differences and allocate time for individual thinking. For everyone, even for the most talkative extroverts, it is good to just sit down in silence and think; there will be more ideas and the logic behind ideas gets stronger. Also, if you jump directly into group discussion, the first opinions tend to have an anchoring effect on new ideas and the ideas tend to become similar. The individual stage helps groups produce a more diverse set of ideas to begin with.

The amount of time given for the individual stage depends on the complexity and number of potential ideas. If I am leading an actioning session where people are expected to think of specific tasks related to a simple process, then one or two minutes of time for the individual stage is enough. If I am conducting a creativity session where ideas are more abstract and complex, around 5-10 minutes for the individual stage is fine. And sometimes even more time is needed for the individual stage, like when people are asked to try to explain and map out their own logic.

Stage 2: Steal with Pride

In this stage the facilitator introduces the ground rule, *steal with pride*, and places people into small groups.

The ground rule *steal with pride* gives permission to take other people's ideas. I typically explain that this would involve participants sharing their ideas, inquiring about the ideas of others, and then developing ideas together. In the small group discussions the ideas lose ownership and become common property of the group. This begins to create group consensus.

I've been asked more than once by facilitators if this ground rule could be worded more softly because participants might resist the idea of stealing. For some, the world steal has strong, negative connotations. People are taught from a young age not to steal, and some of us may have heard a story about a person who lost their job or ruined their career due to theft related reasons. In the ground rule of Idealogue, the word steal can be replaced with something softer like *take* or *exchange* if need be, but I have to say that "exchange ideas with pride" does not have the same ring to it.

While these doubts about the word steal may be worrying in theory, when using Idealogue in practice the participants never resist stealing. I told a facilitator friend of mine about Idealogue and that I was about to facilitate a session in Florida for a group of women that work in the public sector. My friend told me, "Pepe, the moment you tell them to steal with pride, they are going to throw you out of the room. The whole concept of stealing is against everything they represent and it just isn't going to work."

Luckily for me my friend was completely wrong, and the group of little old ladies had no problem following my instructions of 'steal with pride.' No one complained and everyone was happy. People like to have others listen to their ideas. People even like to have others take their ideas. I am not talking about stealing the plans for some new multi-million dollar invention. We all want to be influential and to have an impact. Being influential is having your ideas understood, accepted and then passed on by others to a larger audience.

> **Steal with Pride**
> - Gives permission to take ideas from others, making ideas shared property of the group.
>
> **Collect the best ideas on your own piece of paper**
> - Individual competitive task with a clear objective
> - In order to steal the best ideas you have to understand what the best ideas are; this makes people ask the magic question "why?" and understanding of ideas gets deeper.

Figure 9: Two key concepts of Idealogue.

A key instruction I give to the group during this stage is to *collect the best ideas on your own piece of paper*. This is the very core of the method and relates directly to the ground rule *steal with pride*. If I asked the participants to share, that would be a group task without an individual objective. If at this stage I asked the participants to agree on the best ideas, I would have a group arguing about what the best ideas are before they have had a chance to understand them.

Asking the group to collect the best ideas for themselves and on their own piece of paper makes it an individual task, and it makes each participant personally responsible to fulfil it. It has a clear goal and it is motivating. Also, there is no need to argue about the best solutions. If you find something that you consider to be a good idea you write it on your own paper, then you simply move on to the next idea.

The method shines because it is impossible to write down other people's ideas without first understanding them. This forces the participants to find out what logic lies behind ideas. People ask the important question, "why?" They are forced to think about the ideas in broader contexts and on a deeper level.

When I divide people into small groups, I instruct them simply to form groups of three. Why groups of three? Sometimes pair discussion just does not work. Based on my long experience working with groups around the world, I have seen people working in pairs struggle to maintain conversation. When you have more than three participants the silent ones tend to drop out of conversation and just fly under the radar. In groups of three you typically have enough diversity of ideas and shy or quiet people feel comfortable enough to participate without feeling overwhelmed. In most cases you can't have only groups of three because the number of participants cannot be divided by three. In that case you may have some groups of two or four.

> ## Steal with Pride !
> - Collect best ideas on your own piece of paper
> - Talk, listen, develop
> - Work in groups of three
>   12 minutes

Figure 10: Instructions for stealing with pride.

The amount of time spent on this stage depends on the complexity of the session's context. A typical round of stealing takes about ten to twelve minutes. However, I have held creativity sessions where technical experts were sharing and discussing ideas for almost two hours in groups of three until we formed new groups to repeat the stealing process.

Stage 3: Repeated Stealing

New groups of three are formed and the ideas are further developed.

The simplest way of forming new groups is just to tell the participants to stand up and quickly find two new people to form a group with.

Why do we repeat the stealing stage again in different small groups? It is repeated again in order to further promote the exchange and comprehension of ideas. The first group of three now has a good understanding of each other's ideas and probably even a common understanding of the best ideas. But they don't understand what else is happening in the room, so you have to connect the first group and their ideas with the ideas of other groups by repeated sharing.

Idealogue is a consensus creating method. The more times people form new groups to share, the better understanding you create within the whole group. I sometimes joke that you have to keep changing groups and having people share again and again until the point of exhaustion, so that they are tired and will agree with just about anything! In practice I don't try to tire the group out quite that much, and I typically have three to four rounds of sharing in small groups. Anything past this and we reach a point of diminishing returns; the energy starts going down as people get a little tired of talking, thinking and developing each other's ideas.

If the first round of sharing takes ten minutes, you should give a bit more time for the subsequent rounds. This is because after each round of sharing, people have more to talk about due to the ideas that they have stolen from others. On average about ten to fifteen minutes per round should be fine.

A lot of the time I place an individual stage of idea development between each round of stealing. In between stealing sessions I tell the group something like this: "Now take a careful look at your precious list of ideas, develop them and create new ones. You have four minutes."

I am just a strong believer on giving people an opportunity to think. We do not think enough! Well, at least I don't.

Stage 4: Ideas Selection

At this stage people remain in small groups and select the best ideas. Once a group has agreed on what the best ideas are, they post them at the front of the room so everyone can see what they came up with. The previous stages had an individual focus; to collect best ideas on your own piece of paper. Now the participants should seek agreement and consensus, which should come relatively easy after rounds of stealing and creating understanding of the logic behind ideas.

Choose the best ideas !
- Try to reach consensus.
- The number of ideas chosen is not limited but there can't be too many "best ideas".
- Write ideas down in large lettering on a piece of paper.
- When your group is ready, post the ideas in front of the room for everyone to see.
- 12 minutes

Figure 11: Instructions for choosing ideas.

The number of chosen ideas is not limited. You just can't ask participants to post a specific number of ideas, it is crucial that they are not limited at all during the selection stage by such requirements. What if the group has five excellent ideas or just one? Instead of forcing the group to agree on a certain number of ideas I ask them to simply post the best ideas. However, I often remind participants that all ideas can't be considered best, so they do need to reduce the total number of ideas.

Here is a small hint. Make sure that the groups have materials to write the ideas down in large lettering. Small post-it notes will not do. They need to be written on large pieces of paper in thick marker so that they can be seen by everyone at the same time. About fifteen minutes should be fine for choosing ideas.

Stage 5: Ideas Evaluation

During this stage the facilitator makes sure that the entire group understands the posted ideas by giving time for questions as needed. After it is clear that the ideas are understood, the group as a whole can evaluate them.

Interestingly, the participants do not need to present the ideas they posted with their small groups because a shared understanding of these ideas already exists on a group level. The repetition of group formation in the previous stages has guaranteed increased and inquisitive dialogue which contributes favorably to the chances of arriving at an understanding of the ideas. It is the facilitator who has not participated in group work who is tempted to hear long boring presentations of the ideas that everyone is already familiar with. It is enough to ask the group to read all ideas in silence and if some of the ideas are not understood, you may elaborate and reply to any questions.

At this stage many facilitators like to group ideas. Grouping or organizing the ideas beyond this point is not needed. I am an enemy of grouping ideas, and I will explain why by using the topic of what to have for dinner as an example. Pretend you are trying to make a decision on what you are going to have as main course for dinner. Your friends have suggested salmon, beef, perch, lamb, pork, and cod. Now you group the different suggestions as meat and fish. This will not help decision making at all. When you group ideas you lose the real content and it makes decision making more difficult. When defining a problem grouping can even be dangerous. You group the problem, it becomes something else and you cannot see the real problem anymore. Also, grouping ideas can be difficult due to people trying to group things that do not really belong together, which can lead to unnecessary arguing. However, you may group the ideas if there are a lot of ideas posted. Sometimes organizing ideas into groups can be useful to create an outline which may be easier to understand than a large number of individual ideas.

Now it is crucial to evaluate the results. For instance, if you are clarifying the problem, you ask the group: "do we have the problem here?" If you are creating a common vision, you inquire whether the group feels that the vision is common. If you have created new ideas, you ask whether the ideas meet the goals of the creativity session. And if you have created an action plan, you want to make sure the actions cover all the solutions you have agreed before actioning. And what if the group is not happy with all ideas? Then you ask for new ideas. For instance, you may have one more round of small group work in groups of three, with the discussion topic being how to improve the results of the session.

A typical Idealogue session takes about an hour and a half and consists of; introduction and focusing for 15 minutes, the individual ideas phase for 5 minutes, stealing with pride in changing small groups for 45 minutes, choosing and posting the best ideas for 15 minutes, discussion for 10 minutes, one or two minutes to evaluate the results and get group feedback, and finally another minute or so to thank the group and end the session. The length of the session can vary depending on the number of participants and the topic. The longest Idealogue session I have been a part of was a creativity session which lasted about 5 hours.

Idealogue is perfect for groups ranging from 6 to 24 participants, although it can be used effectively with larger groups too. In very small groups you may have to use pairs instead of groups of three. Ideologue has been successfully used in groups of hundreds of participants. Even in a large group setting it will help people develop their ideas. However, in large groups building consensus becomes harder simply due to the number of connections that exist between participants.

In a workshop Idealogue can be used to clarify a message, problem or goal. It also can be used in creativity sessions and the action planning stage of a workshop. You will find more about how to use Idealogue in following chapters.

Stage 1: Individual stage
- Participants are asked to write down their ideas in silence

Stage 2: Steal with pride
- At this stage, the facilitator introduces the ground rule and small groups of three participants are formed
- Steal with Pride!
- Collect the best ideas on your own piece of paper
- Share, listen, and develop ideas

Stage 3: Repeated stealing
- New groups of three are formed and the second stage is repeated several times

Stage 4: Ideas selection
- At this stage, the participants remain in groups of three and select the best ideas
- Choose the best ideas
- Try to reach consensus
- Write down best ideas on a piece of paper with a marker
  (The number is not limited but just the best ideas can't be many)
- One idea per paper
- When your group is ready post your ideas on the wall

Stage 5: Ideas evaluation
- The facilitator makes sure the group understands the posted ideas and the participants evaluate the results

Stage 1: Individual stage

- Participants are asked to write down their ideas in silence.

Stage 2: Steal with pride

- At this stage, the facilitator introduces the ground rule and small groups of three participants are formed.
- Steal with Pride!
- Collect the best ideas on your own piece of paper
- Share, listen, and develop ideas

Stage 3: Repeated stealing

- New groups of three are formed and the second stage is repeated several times.

Stage 4: Ideas selection

- At this stage, the participants remain in groups of three and select the best ideas.
- Choose the best ideas
- Try to reach consensus
- Write down best ideas on a piece of paper with a marker (The number is not limited but best ideas cannot be many)
- One idea per paper
- When your group is ready post your ideas on the wall

Stage 5: Ideas evaluation

- The facilitator makes sure the group understands the posted ideas and the participants evaluate the results.

Figure 12: The stages of Idealogue.

Chapter 4

Visioning

Idealogue is suitable for use in common business situations and it can be, and sometimes should be used with other facilitation tools. I believe that the best way to demonstrate this is to see Idealogue in action.

A Phone Call from Lagos

One great thing about my job as a facilitator is that I am never bored. In my almost twenty years as a facilitator, I have had the pleasure to meet thousands of people working in all types of industries and businesses. I have been able to learn about ways of working and experience new cultures. And I have spent entirely too much time in airports and on planes, a small disadvantage to the great opportunities I have had to travel all around the world, facilitating as I go. I think the best part of this job is that the demands and the working environments are constantly changing, and I never know where facilitation will be needed next. The same can be said for Idealogue: it can be used in a variety of different contexts. I can easily remember the phone call which led me to take my first ever trip to Africa.

Lagos? I'm pretty sure that is Nigeria, I thought to myself as my phone identified the city associated with the +234-1 area code which was flashing on the screen.

After I answered with a brief "Hello, this is Pepe", the voice on the other end got right down to business.

"Hello Pepe, my name is Esther and I am calling on behalf of Sam Adebayo of Assorted Nigerian Limited."

After thanking Esther for the call and asking her how I could assist her and the company she represented, Esther explained to me how Assorted Nigerian Limited is a manufacturing company which makes a variety of products in their factories that are located in different regions of Nigeria.

"There is very little overlap in what each factory produces. Our factory here in Lagos makes children's toys, and up North in Kano we are producing pet food and tires. In the whole country we have six factories, each focused on a different product. The management teams in each factory are completely focused on their own products, and have little to no interaction with the other factories. Because of this, there are many misunderstandings when all of the managers come together for companywide meetings. Our company president and CEO Mr. Adebayo feels like he is stuck in the middle of everything and has to mediate all of these conflicts. The company is willing to spend some time and resources in defining common strategic goals, and we want you to help us."

I thanked Esther for considering me for the job, and I accepted. We continued chatting a while longer on the phone as we continued to plan out the details of the upcoming session. Esther mentioned on the phone there was not a lot of teamwork between factory managers, and there definitely were not any shared goals or a unified company vision.

I told her that I thought it would be best to first create a common vision with the leadership team, and then continue with strategizing, and finally make an action plan that would provide the workable steps to follow through on the new, shared company vision and strategies. But more about strategizing and actioning later, let's not get ahead of ourselves. With Assorted Nigeria Limited, we need to start by visioning.

Getting Started on the Right Foot

About two weeks after my first conversation with Esther, I was in a conference room attached to a fancy hotel in downtown Lagos. I had never been to this city of 20 million before, and I was grateful that the conference room was actually attached to the very same hotel that I was staying in, as I had heard stories about Lagos' legendarily awful traffic. As I readied the room I was curious about what it would be like working with Assorted Nigeria Limited. *I hope that these people are OK with disagreement* I thought. Having never worked with Assorted Nigerian Limited, let alone in Nigeria, I did not know what to expect from the company culture, or the national culture. In some places conflict is embraced and encouraged and in others it can grow to become the giant elephant in the corner of the room that no one talks about but everyone is affected by. I had these things on my mind as I finished organizing the nine chairs into a semi-circle facing the front of the room when everyone walked in.

The leader of the group was Sam Adebayo, the CEO and acting president of Assorted Nigeria Limited. He spoke quietly but firmly, and was dressed in a nice suit, as Nigerian business culture dictated. Next was Esther, the woman who was Sam's right hand man so to speak. She was the COO of the company, but was also constantly giving feedback to Sam, as he tended to run most tough business decisions by her before taking action. Then there was Ade, a small, seemingly quiet guy with glasses, he was the Chief Financial Officer of the company.

The rest of the group was rounded out by the managers of the production factories for Assorted Nigerian Limited. Since the company did not have any specific specialization, but instead let opportunity and market conditions dictate what they produced, the location of the factories, their size, and the products produced varied greatly.

As they entered the room and offered up a handshake, they greeted me with their name, factory location and the product that their factory specialized in.

"Hello, I am John Ambrose from the Lagos pet food factory."

"Moses Simon from Kano, textiles."

"Hello Pepe, I am Cecilia from the Abuja factory specializing in rubber tire valves."

"A pleasure to meet you. Wilfred from the largest children's toy factory in Lagos."

"Hi, My name is Alex Musa, and I manage the Ibadan pen factory."

"Nice to meet you Pepe, I am Eve Ebi, and I run the cosmetics factory based in Lagos."

Despite the infighting and poor communication between the company managers, confidence was not a problem as everyone seemed to be proud of the goods their factory produced.

"It is very nice to be here and meet all of you" I said to the group, as they settled into their chairs.

"I am very happy I was invited to Lagos. Look at this weather today; beautiful, sunny, and 28 degrees Celsius. This time of year in Helsinki it is dark 20 hours of the day and the temperature is well below freezing. So once again I say from the bottom of my heart, thanks for the invitation."

With the introductions taken care of, it was time to warm the group up, and elicit their expectations for the day's session. To do this I told them to spend a minute to think about the current situation of the company and what they hoped to accomplish today. After letting everyone think this over, I told them to share their ideas with a partner. Once they had done this, the entire group was brought back together and I asked everyone to quickly share their partner's expectations.

Although I was interested in what their expectations were, this activity served a more important purpose. It relaxes participants and gets them comfortable working with other people and speaking in groups, two things which they will need to do extensively throughout the rest of the session.

The Expectations for the Day
- Sam: To all get on the same page and establish better communication.
- Esther: Develop a common vision for Assorted Nigeria Ltd.
- Ade: Prioritize upcoming projects based on importance.
- John: Stop company waste and pointless spending.
- Moses: Try a new method to fix our old problems.
- Cecilia: A free lunch. Besides that, not much. (quite negative)
- Wilfred: No expectations, but an open mind.
- Alex: Gain trust in teammates.
- Eve: Learn about other managers, learn to work together.

Figure 13: The expectations of the Assorted Nigeria Ltd. management team.

Also, despite everyone working for the same company, a lot of the Assorted Nigeria Limited managers were not accustomed to speaking and sharing with one another because of the different focuses each factory had, and the scattered locations of the factories. This activity helped break the ice and get them comfortable talking to each other by allowing them to connect with each other. Every facilitation session has a beginning and everyone practicing facilitation principles should recognize the importance of the beginning of the session.

After warming the group up and having everyone share their expectations for the session, it was my turn to fill them in a bit about how the session was structured, and why.

The Vision for the Day

"Today we are here to take part in a visioning session. Do any of you know what a visioning session is or how it works?"

Alex cleared his throat and replied, "I have never participated in this type of session before, but I imagine the goal is to get all of us to agree on what the best vision for Assorted Nigeria Limited is."

I thanked Alex for his comment and explained that visioning is not about convincing somebody to agree with your vision. Instead visioning is about creating a common goal or a future course of action based on the similarities of people's ideas.

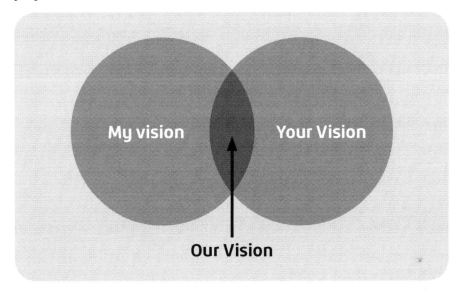

Figure 14: Our Vision: the important space where individual visions and ideas meet and become more.

"What we first want to do is share our own vision with others," I explained as I drew a large circle on the whiteboard and wrote the words *My Vision* inside.

"Next we want to listen to and understand the visions of our colleagues," I said, as I drew another circle next to the first, writing in the words *Your Vision*. "Where the two visions meet is *Our Vision*, and identifying what is in this space is what we are here to do today. If we can strongly define that area and what sort of ideas and visions fall into it, then Assorted Nigeria Limited will find synergy, and collaboration between different factories will seem effortless going forward."

Most of the nine audience members smiled at the thought of improved communication, and even Cecilia, who came into the session with a poor attitude and only expecting "a free lunch and some coffee" seemed intrigued. With the group now warmed up and eager, it was time to begin.

Wishing for a Better Future

"Alright everyone, now we are going to take a moment to make some wishes. Can someone finish the following sentence for me? *It would be great if...*"

As I waited for someone to finish the sentence by making a wish, I wrote "*It would be great if*" on the white paper flipchart at the front of the room.

Ade was the first to finish the sentence. "It would be great if I could do my job without having to spend so much time on paperwork."

Esther shot back, "Ade, you are an accountant! You should have known that you were signing up for a lifetime of paperwork by accepting that job!" Esther then continued on, making her wish: "It would be great if this group got together more often. It has been years since that last time I saw some of you!" she exclaimed, looking towards John and Moses.

Wilfred added, "It would be great if Nigeria would win the World Cup."

Several people cheered in agreement before I continued on with my explanation.

> The wishing activity is used commonly in visioning sessions, or to help a group create goals. Many different "wishing prompts" can be used, with some common ones listed below.
> - I wish...
> - In the future I would like to...
> - Wouldn't it be nice if...
> - It would be fantastic if in ten years...

Figure 15: The wishing activity is used in this example as a starting point for Idealogue.

"Those all are some great wishes. Some of these wishes seem more likely to happen than others, no offence to the Nigerian football team. At least they usually make it to the World Cup. That alone is much more than I can say for my beloved Finland. Anyhow, the wish about the football team is a great one! 'Now you have started wishing, big wishes are not just OK, but encouraged. A wish is not supposed to be logical. Instead, it comes directly from the heart. Something that really makes a difference. These are the types of wishes we trying to make for Assorted Nigerian Limited."

I pointed to the phrase *It would be great if....* that was written already on the flip-chart and I made a small change to it. It now read, *It would be great if in five years Assorted Nigeria Limited....*

"Now instead of wishing on a personal level, I want all of you to take five minutes to come up with the best wishes you can for Assorted Nigeria Limited. There are absolutely no restrictions for what the wishes can be. I only have two guidelines for you. First, you have five minutes to write down your wishes. And second, since this is an individual activity, no talking."

Everyone began to scribble down wishes on their papers, and after a moment Eve Ebi, the manager of the Lagos cosmetics factory was worried.

"Pepe I just don't think that five minutes will be enough time to write everything down. There are simply too many wishes!"

Knowing that I was going to give her extra time if that was necessary, I assured her, and everyone else not to worry about getting everything written down but instead to just write what they can in the five minute time period. As Sam, Esther, Alex, and the rest of the Assorted Nigeria Limited employees wrote down their wishes, I took a moment to walk around the room to see if anyone had any other questions, and also to take a look at some of the wishes that were being written down. Ade's wish was "I wish that sharing resources with other factories and departments would actually feel good." One of John's wishes was for regularly held collaborative meetings that played an important part in Assorted Nigeria Limited's strategy formation. Cecilia strove for excellence and nothing less, wishing that Assorted Nigeria Limited was the undisputed leader in all the markets it entered.

As the five minutes given for this activity were about to run out, I had time to catch a glimpse of Wilfred's paper, where I saw that one of his wishes was for a strong human resources department to develop.

Please Steal with Pride

Everyone seemed satisfied with the wishes they conjured up during the individual stage, and it was now time to start stealing.

"OK everyone! So far, so good. From the few wishes I have seen and from how quickly you all were writing, I am completely confident that you managed to think of some great wishes. But now it is time for the real magic to begin. Now it is time to start stealing with pride!"

After explaining to the group that the purpose was to have the best set of wishes on your own piece of paper and that stealing in this context was not a bad thing, but instead encouraged and that it helped ideas be understood and prioritized[4], I prompted everybody to form groups of three. For this session I decided to let people form their own groups, without any special instructions on how to form the small groups. While sometimes assigning numbers to people and then having groups form based on those numbers is a good method, there were only nine participants for this session, and most of the people did not know each other well. This meant that working with friends or forming cliques was not an issue. Simple, easy to understand and easy to execute instructions were fine in this case.

"OK, look around you and find two additional people to make groups of three. Once your group has been formed, please sit down together and begin stealing wishes with one another."

Three groups of three quickly materialized people began stealing wishes right away. I hardly had time congratulate myself on how well the session was going and proclaim myself the world's greatest facilitator when an argument broke out.

Two loud voices rose above the rest, and they belonged to Cecilia and Moses. Moses, who managed a factory specializing in textiles, had taken exception to something Cecilia had said and was just about to finish the sentence, "that's your wish? Well I have another wish for you then! I wish you would…"

Before Moses could finish and potentially say something that would require a lengthy report from Human Resources, I gently interjected, much to the relief of Eve, who was the third member of Moses' and Cecilia's group.

"Hey you two. Is there something I can help with here?"

"You can try to help, but I am not sure if it will be much use. Cecilia just informed me that her wish basically calls for the eradication and closure of my factory. If she had her way, I would not be a part of this company in five years' time! How can you help with *that* Pepe?"

I turned to Cecilia as she replied, "that's completely untrue. My wish is for Assorted Nigeria Limited to be the market leader in all markets we enter. If you think that this is impossible for you and your textiles, then sorry, but good riddance! Pepe himself said that our wishes should be big, and Wilfred wished earlier for

---

[4] A detailed explanation of the importance of what "stealing with pride" means and the concepts behind it can be found in Chapter 3.

Nigeria to win the bloody World Cup! It is my wish, Moses, and I can make it without you taking offense to it!"

"Cecilia, I take offense because the importance of my factory and textile production is not measured just by being the market leader! We have been third in that market for years and years, but we stay close to the companies ahead of us, and do it at a fraction of what they spend! You should know this, and if you are any sort of business woman you should see why your wish is wrong!"

"My dear friends, we did not come here to argue. If you do not agree with someone's wish, you explain your reasoning to make your point of view understood and you simply do not steal any ideas that you do not like". After smoothing this issue over, people continued working together for a few more minutes before it was time to change groups.

"So far, so good. Now it is time to take the wishes you have stolen and find two new people to steal from. Look around, find two people you have not worked with today, and make new groups of three."

Everyone did a good job quickly following my instructions, and new groups were formed for the second round of idea stealing. The core principle of Idealogue,-*steal with pride*-, was at work, and I could see everyone engaged in enthusiastic discussion. I also heard wishes being debated and refined, giving birth to new wishes.

After a few more minutes had passed, I told everyone to find the remaining two people they have not worked with so that the final incarnation of groups of three could be formed. After a third round of stealing, I told everyone to stay in their current groups, and try to narrow down what the best wishes of the day were. I told them to agree as a group on wishes were the best for Assorted Nigeria Limited. Once they had reached an agreement, they were instructed to write the wishes down on large pieces of paper, and then tape them to a wall at the front of the room.

Within minutes, ten pieces of paper were taped to the wall, each representing an important wish. Everyone took a moment to read to the wishes; they all were quite interested in what the others really wanted for their company.

The best ideas have been produced during repeated conversations during the small group stages of Idealogue. It was time to try and rank these ideas in terms of importance. To pull this off, I thought I would use something that almost everyone loves and can never have enough of: money.

Prioritizing Together

To get the entire group to begin to agree on what the most important and best idea is among those posted at the front of the room, I needed to use a prioritizing tool. I chose to use a favorite of mine which I call the $10 method. In this activity, each group is given $10 which they use to invest in any of the ideas posted at the front of the room. All of their money can go to one idea, it can be divided among several ideas, or, they can even choose not to invest in any ideas if they decide none of them are worth investing in.

"Now you have produced your very best wishes for Assorted Nigeria Limited." I said, as I looked at the posted wishes at the front of the room. "What we need to do now is take things a step further and try to agree on what are the best of these posted wishes."

Before I could continue, John interrupted. "That may be a bit ambitious Pepe. I think you have noticed that the wishes posted at the front of the room are vastly different from one another. One of them is about being more human, another about better communication, and others about performance and quality of goods produced."

John continued, "Making matters more difficult is the fact that all of us are very different too. We work in different markets, and we produce different products. We are united under the Assorted Nigeria Limited banner, but we also work and live in different places too."

"It may not be easy John, but look how far all of you have come in just a few hours. We have not even been together for a whole day, and together the nine of you have already produced the most important wishes for Assorted Nigeria Limited. John, it may look difficult but let's see how it goes, OK"

John agreed, as the rest of the group nodded.

I continued onwards, trying to ease doubt and explain how they would prioritize the best wishes.

"All you need to do now is to find yourself a partner. I am going to give each pair $10 which can be invested among the four wishes posted at the front of the room. There are no rules as to how the money should be invested. All $10 can go to a single wish, or, it can be divided among different wishes. The goal here is to just invest the money into what you think is most important. But you have to agree *as a pair* how the money will be invested, so feel free to discuss, argue, defend and justify your logic behind your investing choice if needed. Since we have an uneven number of participants, there will be one group of three with $15 to invest. *You* all have another twelve minutes for this activity, so please begin."

Voices once again filled the air as deliberations and explanations took place inside each of the pairs. While this took place, I drew a column on the flip chart for each group, so that when they were ready, a representative from that group could write the results so that anyone in the entire room could see.

1. It would be great if in five years the factories and departments of Assorted Nigeria Ltd. were truly united $13
2. It would be great if in five years Assorted Nigeria Ltd. was a key player in every country in Africa $12
3. It would be great if in five years Assorted Nigeria Ltd. would be strong in the human side of business $9
4. It would be great if in five years Assorted Nigeria Ltd. was the quality leader and recognized for the superiority of the goods they produced $7

Figure 16: The investment results of the $10 method; the top four vision elements of Assorted Nigeria Ltd.

One by one, a person from each pair came to the front of the room and wrote their pair's investment decisions on the chart. The results from each group were not identical. This is not what is meant by finding consensus. There were differences in how the wishes were prioritized and how much money was invested in each, but these differences were unimportant. What is important is that there was a common trend of almost all of the money being invested in the wish for a more united company. This is what the $10 method and other similar activities hope to bring out: a shared idea or common trend in thinking, not perfect alignment.

I needed to give the chance for individual feedback regarding these results. Sometimes in small group activities it just takes one strong personality within a group to make decisions on behalf of the other group members. That is why feedback from the entire group is needed to both understand where the group is at, and also to verify that the results of an activity are actually reflective of the group's mindset or views. For the session with Assorted Nigeria Limited, I used the five fingers method, which gave everyone the chance to rate the results of the investment activity on a scale of one to five. I explained to everyone how the five fingers method worked:

"There is a clear concentration of votes on four wishes with just a few dollars on the rest. I call these wishes 'elements of our common vision'. Now, I would like you to evaluate the vision elements and soon I am going to ask you to vote with your fingers. One finger means that you hate them, two fingers that you dislike them, three fingers signifies that you can live with them, four fingers is if you like the vision elements, and five fingers if you love the vision elements."

I then counted to three and asked the participants to show their fingers. All fours and fives were given for the vision elements. Then I called on people to elaborate on why they gave the scores they did.

Sam Adebayo, the big boss spoke up. "I gave five fingers. When I see the four vision elements we all produced at the front of the room, I just love them all. I want the company to be human, I also want our people and assets to be united and work in unison. And what member of our team wouldn't want improved quality and market positioning? I agree that being truly united is the most important though, because achieving that would have a spillover effect and improve the other three wishes."

Sam's colleagues nodded in agreement. Alex was the last one to comment and added, "I gave four fingers. I like those ideas and agree with you Mr. Adebayo, but it is so easy to say we want these things on a day like today, and with the help of a professional like Pepe. But will we even remember these ideas in a week's time? A month?"

Alex's question of if the best ideas produced by the group would even stick around and be remembered and acted on provided the perfect transition to the next activity I had planned for the session, so I jumped in.

Making it memorable

"Thanks to Mr. Adebayo, and also to everyone else your feedback. Addressing your concerns Alex, the difficult work is done. You all have produced some great elements of success that Assorted Nigeria Limited can strive for in the future. Not only that, you all have managed to agree on prioritizing them. That is nothing short of remarkable. But now that you have your vision for the future, we need to make it memorable. It is time to have a bit of fun. I am going to put you into three small groups and give a different creative task for each group based around our chosen vision elements of a more united Assorted Nigeria Limited. Esther, pick two pleasant colleagues, your group is going to write a vision statement combining all of the vision elements for Assorted Nigeria Limited."

Esther and her group members wasted no time, and got right down to work.

"Wilfred, Moses, and Cecilia, your group is going to write and perform a short play that shows what the vision elements look like for Assorted Nigeria Limited employees in five years."

Wilfred and his group members began brainstorming ideas for their short play, laughing.

The remaining group looked skeptical, wondering just how creative they were going to have to get. I pulled out a large box of Legos, which answered their questions immediately.

"And you all get to channel your inner children and do some building with these Lego blocks. How can the new vision elements be represented by using these?"

I think that they may have been a bit taken aback by what I was asking of them, but since the objective of the activity was explained to them, they understood the point of what they were being instructed to do, making it easier for them to follow instructions.

With the instructions given, I took a moment to stand back and watch the groups at work. Legos were being clicked into place, pens scribbled down vision statements for the future, and long dormant acting skills were re-emerging. After about half an hour, I called everyone together once more.

"Now the fun part. Let's see what you all came up with. Which group would like to present first?"

One by one each of the groups came to the front of the room to show the fruits of their labors. The group responsible for making a short play about the vision elements acted out a scene where a factory in the South has a machine fail in the middle of fulfilling an order. Within hours, employees from other factories are trying to help out and relieve the pressure by working overtime. Replacement parts are in the mail, sent from a Northern factory which had the parts needed to make the repair.

After this was acted out, applause and laughter filled the room. Next, the Lego architects came to the front, holding a large Lego platform. John, one of the Lego builders, explained his group's creation.

"If you all look closely, you will see six green buildings. All of these represent the factories spread around Nigeria. This larger building is where Sam, Esther and Ade are based, the company headquarters in Lagos. And now the magic of it all. See these lines that run every-which way? These are our connections as a company. They run from factory to factory and also every other direction as well. Look, this one is pointed to the sky. The point is that we are unified not just with each other, but to our country, and foreign African markets as well."

Again a round of applause was given. Finally the vision statement of the future was given by the last remaining group. Esther cleared her throat and read, "Assorted Nigeria Limited is the crowned eagle of the African market: Soaring above the competition as a unified family."

Cheers rang about room. Sam Adebayo was especially excited, shouting, "that's wonderful you guys! I want to put that up on our website immediately!"

I must admit that I felt a bit out of the loop. I had never heard of the crowned eagle before and to me, it sounded like something that belonged in a J.R.R. Tolkien novel. I did not understand why this particular statement was so well received, so I asked.

"Pepe", said Sam. "Do you know what the national bird of Nigeria is?"

I admitted that I did not.

"It is the crowned eagle. It holds a special significance in our country."

Wilfred, the fanatical football fan who wished for a Nigerian World Cup championship chimed in; "and our national sports teams are almost always called the eagles too! It's a great symbol for us as a company!"

I was beginning to understand more when Esther explained the rest of the statement.

"We all know about the bird as a national symbol, but do you all know what makes this bird so special?"

No one outside of Esther's group seemed to have a clue.

Esther pushed onwards. "The crowned eagle, our national symbol, is special because it spends much more time together as a family. Most other birds, even other eagles, only lay eggs and feed the small birds for a few months. But the crowned eagle? About a year and a half! We all decided as a group that we want to be more united together. We want to be working together and soaring above our competitors. We, as a company want to be like the crowned eagle!"

The groups sharing what they had produced during the last exercise of the day was a great high note to end on. I knew that the image of a unified group of eagles soaring high above Lagos, dropping Assorted Nigeria Limited products from their beaks would not leave my mind for a while, and I was confident that the important vision of a more unified Assorted Nigeria Limited was going to stay in the minds of the participants as well.

Analysis: What Happened Here?

The objective of my work session with Assorted Nigeria Limited was to outline what it was that the leadership team wanted for their company's future. What were their visions for what Assorted Nigeria Limited should be? Before any specific tools or activities were used, I made sure to define to the group what a common vision is. The visions, which I elicited in the form of wishes, did not need to conform 100% to one another. A visioning session does not seek to force all members of the group to think the same. Instead, the shared similarities and common ground between visions is what is being looked for. It is important to explain this to the group in the beginning to avoid possible arguments when participants are trying to force each other to accept ideas that may not prove, in the end, to be very important. Also, common ground is what can be used in future sessions to form a strategy and actionable points to transform these visions from wishes to reality.

What Tools Were Used?

I used a combination of tools when running the visioning session with Assorted Nigeria Limited. By doing this, I hoped to achieve a few things. First, I hoped to create an environment where people could begin to express their visions. Sometimes it can be a challenge to get someone to look past the present moment and into the future, especially if there are problems that are present in the current working environment.

I prompted everyone to express their visions for the company by using the wishing activity. Everyone can relate to making a wish, as many people grow up with stories about genies and fairy godmothers granting wishes. In many parts of the world, people make wishes on their birthday or at the start of a new year, so I find that the activity is intuitive and a good vehicle with which people can express future visions for their company or working life.

The wishing activity also took place as an individual activity, which meant that work could be done at a speed that was comfortable for everyone, and there was no pressure of conversation during the activity.

Once the wishes were produced individually, stolen and posted during the group phase, I used the invest $10 activity as a prioritization tool. The aim of investing $10 is to get people to agree on what the most important ideas (in this case wishes or visions for the future) were. In the invest $10 activity, the group can decide to assign value to the ideas however they wish or they may even decide not to invest anything. I always have participants prioritize in pairs or small groups in order to make sure they will have a good talk about the value of ideas one more time.

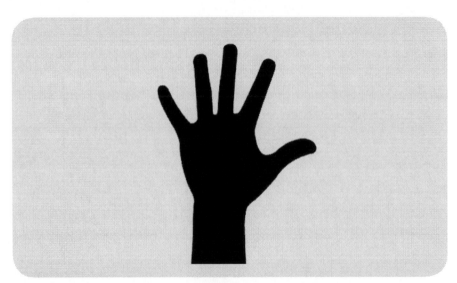

Figure 17: The five fingers method. 1 finger: I hate it. 2 fingers: I don't like it. 3 fingers: It's Ok/I can live with it. 4 fingers: I like it. 5 fingers: I love it!

Getting Feedback from the Group

It is also important for me as the facilitator to make sure that I understand the group's understanding and feelings regarding the selected ideas, so I always take time to elicit feedback from the group. One way to do this is the *five fingers* tool. I first make sure that I have the attention of the entire group. Then I ask them to think about their feelings concerning the ideas selected by the group. Do they support these ideas? I then instruct people to raise their hands in the air, and hold up either one, two, three, four or five fingers, depending on their feelings. Five fingers means complete support or agreement; that they love the results and the content produced could not have been better. Four fingers means that they like it, while three fingers signifies "OK", or that they can live with the idea. Two fingers means that they dislike the content and just one finger in the air indicates very strong disagreement or hate. When using the five fingers tool, I am not hoping for complete group agreement. On the contrary, I hope to see a variety of responses. The aim of this exercise is to elicit feedback from the group and allow for people to express their differing opinions. Sometimes in the group work stages, especially the idea selection and group consensus stage, strong personalities can dominate, pushing others to the sidelines. The five fingers activity gives everyone a chance to be heard, and if the group is not happy with the results, we can backtrack to the idea selection phase or discuss together or in small groups the produced content.

When all fingers are up, I ask participants to guess the average based on what they see in order to get an idea of the group opinion. I then ask one of the "fives" to comment. This is then repeated with the "fours", and then the "threes", "twos" and finally the "ones".

Using the five fingers tool lets me know how everyone was feeling about the results. On one hand, the content produced by the group lets me know as a facilitator how things went, but this would be an incomplete picture without using a tool like five fingers to get feedback on an individual level[5].

Before the session could end, there still was one more important thing to do, which was assign creativity tasks to each small group. The point of these tasks is not just to laugh and have fun, but to make the day's content memorable. Great conversations can be had for hours on end, but it is much easier to forget an idea expressed in words than it is to forget an idea expressed in a play or a large Lego sculpture.

Each small group was also assigned a different creativity task. This was so that there would be no feeling of competition between the groups. The idea was not to create *the best* Lego sculpture, but simply to create. This alleviates pressure and lets people have fun. It also makes it easier for people to pay attention during the presentation of these ideas. Each group is presenting the same idea, so it can be repetitive, which is good. Repetition also ensures understanding, internalization, and remembrance. The different vehicles which were the play, the Lego sculpture, and the vision statement, entertain and hold everyone's attention.

- Defining a common vision: To make sure everyone was on the same page before beginning.
- Wishing activity: Intuitive, everyone has made a wish before, a good way to get people to share passions, big dreams.
- Idealogue: The backbone, creates a common understanding.
- $10 Investment activity: To prioritize ideas. Used preferably in pairs or small groups to increase understanding.
- Five Fingers: To Evaluate results, hear feedback on individual level.
- Vision statement, building and acting the vision: To make content memorable.

Figure 18: The tools used in the visioning session and the reasons behind their selection.

---

[5] More information about the importance of feedback and using the five fingers activity can be found at the end of Chapter 3.

Why Idealogue?

Behind the effectiveness of the wishing activity, the $10 investment activity, and the creativity tasks, is Idealogue. It serves as the backbone to the other tools, providing support and strengthening their effectiveness.

The goal of the day was finding a common ground relating to people's strategic visions. Idealogue allows for individual idea generation and then promotes repeated dialogue based around those ideas. *Steal with pride* encourages people to understand an idea before they can decide to take it or leave it. Breaking up groups and then reforming other small groups ensures that ideas are refined through constant sharing and stealing. All of this means that the overlapping areas between visions are expanded. As ideas are shared, refined, and stolen, the separate spaces of *my* vision and *your vision* shrink, while group consensus in the form of *our vision* grows.

Chapter 5
Problem Solving

Setting the Stage

The next example takes us to Beijing, China, where we drop in at the headquarters of Soundless Components, a company that makes the internal speakers and assorted gadgetry that are used in the noise cancelling headphones made by larger, more well-known electronics companies worldwide. Soundless components is a diverse company, with three production plants in China, and offices in its founding country of Germany. Soundless Components needs some help. The company has called together fifteen managers and department heads for a problem solving session hosted by an outside consultant, a facilitator named Pepe. The session aims to find a cause for the recent decline in production that has been a trend in their three production facilities.

It is here we are first introduced to Harry Cheung, the Chief Operations Officer for Soundless components, and this chapter's protagonist. As the other participants file into the meeting room, Harry is concerned.

I still don't understand how another meeting and idea session proposes to fix a production problem, Harry thinks to himself as he drinks his morning coffee. *If our factories are producing less, then we need to motivate our workers to do more or budget in more working hours for them, not schedule inter-department chat sessions here at company headquarters.* Harry diverts himself from these thoughts just long enough to smile and wave at Lisa Zhu, from accounting, and Mike Weiss, a sales manager based in Frankfurt. They wave back as Harry returns to his musings. *At least I get to see some people who usually are only at headquarters during the annual holiday party. Oh look, there's Linka from the HR department. This whole 'facilitation' meeting was her idea…at least I know who to blame when things go wrong.* This last thought makes Harry feel a little bit better about the situation.

As Harry continues to scan the room, looking at the others who have been summoned to this meeting, his eyes fall on a face that is not familiar to him. *That must be the facilitator himself* thinks Harry, as the stranger stands up and greets the room.

"Good morning! How is everyone doing today? My name is Pepe, I am a facilitator, and I am here to help out today. First of all, I want to thank you all for inviting me here. It is very nice to be in Beijing. Beijing is a bit like Helsinki, Finland, where I am from. Both places are in the north, and both are beautiful cities…although maybe the food is a bit more flavourful and better here."

"There is no 'maybe' about it!" shouts Lisa Zhu.

This draws smiles from the group. Even Mr Yen, the current president of Soundless Components grins, as Pepe continues.

"As I understand it, you are here today to try and figure out the causes of a production decline, right?"

"I can save us all a bit of time in figuring out what is causing the problem. We already know what it is. The production workers themselves are the problem," says a voice. It was Jeremy Stephens, the head of Public Relations.

Immediately Benjamin Lin, the manager of the production plants in China took exception to this. "Oh come on Jeremy, the problem is not nearly as simple as that! My workers have been working hard and will continue to do a fine job!"

Pepe jumped in. "Well, I am happy to see you all are passionate and enthusiastic about discussing this, and since you seem to have different opinions on what is causing the troubles, this session seems to make sense. If you do not agree on what the cause of the production decline is, you are not going to be able to solve anything. Is it fair to say that the issue you want to solve today is a decline in production in the factories?"

Benjamin, Jeremy, and the rest of the group nodded in agreement as Pepe wrote "production decline" on a large white piece of paper that was on a flip chart at the front of the room.

Using Root Cause Analysis

"In front of you there are sheets of paper and pens. First, start by writing down the issue we are here to discuss today; production decline. It may be easy to think of production decline as the problem that needs solving, but I don't think it is. I think it is a symptom of a larger problem, a core problem that is causing it. Much like a runny nose is an unwanted by-product of having the flu, the decline in production is just an unwanted effect of a larger problem. In order to identify this core problem first think about the reasons why Soundless Components is experiencing a production decline. What causes this problem? What are the factors behind the production decline? There are no right or wrong answers, just think about the issue as you see it and go from there. When you come up with a reason, write it on your paper below production decline, and then draw an arrow connecting the two. Since the reason below production decline causes it, the arrow will point towards "production decline". This creates a second level of understanding below the original problem we want to solve. Then go a level further and think about what causes this new reason. When you have something in mind, write it down below. Continue thinking of new causes and work your way downwards.

There are always more than just one or two factors that cause an issue, so it is OK to have multiple downward columns below the issue of production decline. And the different reasons for production decline in the different columns can be related to one another, and connected with arrows. If you find something related to another idea or cause in your paper, draw an arrow connecting the two. You can draw multiple arrows linking multiple aspects as you see fit. This is *your* logic and *your* work. If it makes sense logically to you, go ahead and put it down on your paper. This exercise is called a *current reality tree*, and it is a type of root cause analysis. What root cause analysis does is allow us to get a sense of the bigger picture, and in this case maybe give us some new ideas about what is causing the production decline. Right now, this is a purely individual task, so no talking. Take about ten minutes to do this. I will let you know when the time is up, and we can return together as a group. Are there any questions at the moment?"

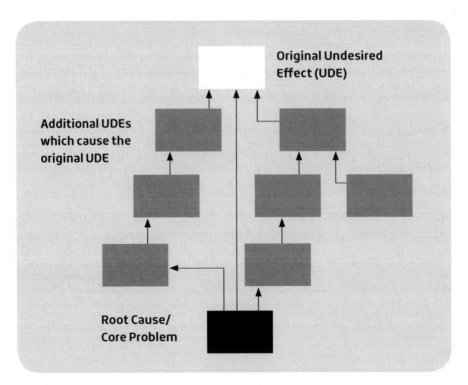

Figure 19: A sample current reality tree; notice that multiple columns are OK and that the core cause has multiple outward arrows flowing from it.

One hand shoots up. It is Doris, from Research and Development, wanting to know how many causes for production decline they are expected to think of.

"Thank you for your question, Doris," says Pepe. "In a typical root cause analysis exercise, it takes about five levels of analysis until you reach the true cause of the problem, the root cause. A good way to tell if you are close is if you end up with a general belief or attitude. A lot of the time beliefs and attitudes form the root cause of the problem, rather than a specific reason. But you do not need to worry right now about how many levels of analysis you should be doing. Are there any other questions? If not, go ahead and get started."

Harry looks down at his piece of paper with the words "production decline" written on it and thinks about the session so far. He is not completely sold on it, but he is not quite ready to lose hope and blame Linka for bringing in the facilitator either. *Everyone seems to have a lot to write down...even the company president Mr. Yen is scribbling away. I guess I will start too.*

Harry circled the words "production decline" and drew a line downwards as he thought about the issue. Before the session began, Harry thought that decreased production was a direct cause of decreased worker output, but as he began to make a current reality tree, he found that he was beginning to think differently about the problem. As the Chief Operations Officer for Soundless Components, Harry sacrificed a lot of his time, energy, and inner-peace to the construction and balancing of company budgets, so he naturally thought that this issue was a financial one. *The production is hindered by re-occurring issues we have with sourcing the materials we need for the components.* Harry wrote in the words "re-occurring sourcing issues", circled them, and drew another line downwards. *What is causing these re-occurring sourcing issues? We cannot stick to a single reliable supplier, and instead we are spending our blasted time always looking for the lowest possible price. Hmm, I guess that is two reasons…maybe I will add another column.* Harry wrote in "Current suppliers unreliable" on his paper and also created a new column by writing "Always changing suppliers. *We are always bargain hunting because company policy prioritizes conservative financial practice* as he continued writing. *And the reason the current suppliers are unreliable is because they are the cheapest possible!*

Harry's hand raced furiously, trying to keep up with his thoughts. After a few more moments of work, Harry thought he had identified the root cause, which was that the company was scared to spend money, which he had written down at the bottom of his paper. Now that he had reached this conclusion, it seemed obvious, but he also was surprised by his own idea.

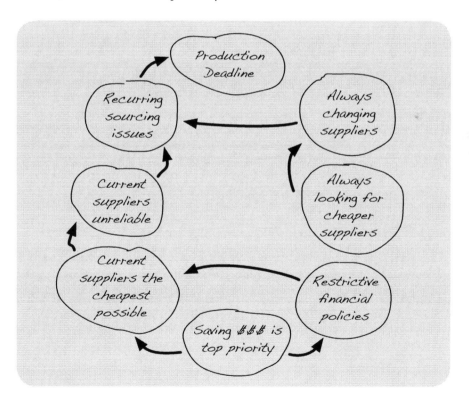

Figure 20: Harry's Current Reality Tree.

As Harry looked up, he could see that the others were just about done as well.

Pepe called for everyone's attention as he gave the next set of instructions to the Soundless Components employees.

"Great Job so far! I see that all of you have written a lot. Maybe we should just stop here and call it a day?"

All fifteen of Soundless Components employees laugh, well almost all of them.

"Stop here? With all due respect Pepe, I don't think you have what it takes to work in China. Here we do not stop until the job is finished."

"Come on Lisa, he was joking," informs Mr. Yen, gesturing for Pepe to continue.

"It looks like all of you have succeeded in identifying the root cause behind the production decline. Great work. But you are not done yet. Knowing the root cause is useful and interesting, but is not what we are looking for. Instead, we want to find the most important problems that you have the power to influence. To find this, I want you to think about your role within Soundless Components. Take your piece of paper with the current reality tree and draw a circle around all the things that you can change. Once you have done this, you will have a circle drawn somewhere on your current reality tree. This circle is called the *sphere of influence*. We are not looking for every single area you can influence, but instead the area that is most relevant to production decline.

Benjamin interrupted Pepe with a question:

"Marking what we can influence is straight-forward enough, but how can we decide what is the most pertinent to the original problem? Wouldn't we just be guessing?"

"Thank you for your question Benjamin. There is actually a very easy way to identify what is most important and impactful to the entire system. Remember all of the arrows you drew connecting cause to another? Look for the issues and problems with the most arrows coming from it. The more arrows, the larger the impact that specific aspect typically has on the whole system, meaning the more important it is. Please take a moment to identify your sphere of influence and the most important thing within the sphere of influence. That is the specific problem that you can use as a starting point for solution building and that is what I want you to find now."

Harry thought a moment while looking at his current reality tree, and realized that within his sphere of influence, the box containing "restrictive financial policies" had the most arrows coming out of it. As COO, this was something he could directly affect, although prior to today, he would have never thought that it could have been linked to the production decline.

Time to Steal

"Now that we all have our own ideas written down, here comes the fun part. Your job now is to steal the best ideas from everyone else. Talk with your colleagues and find out what they came up with as the cause for the decrease in production. When you hear an idea that you think is worth stealing, write it down."

"Do we also write down who the idea comes from?" The question came from Jeremy Stephens, the company's Public Relations officer.

"Great question Jeremy. Do not worry one bit about who you get the idea from, just take it! Normally we are taught not to steal and I agree with this advice most of the time, but not now. Steal with pride! Add the best ideas to your list. Again, all you should be concerned with is getting the best ideas down onto your piece of paper. There are fifteen of you participating so what we are going to do first is to get into groups of three. I will quickly assign a number to each of you and then you all can stand and find the other two people with the same number."

After Pepe had assigned the numbers and fifteen minutes for stealing ideas, everyone stood, and shuffled around, trying to find their group mates as quickly as they could. In less than a minute the task was completed, and what sounded like a dozen different conversations began at once.

Harry found himself grouped with Benjamin who is a manager of a production factory in Guangzhou, and with Barbara, the company's Sales Department leader. Barbara cut right to the chase, demanding that Benjamin and Harry "Hurry up and spill the beans on anything worth stealing, or quit wasting time."

Wow, she really is embracing this 'steal with pride' idea Harry thought, as he began to explain his ideas. Benjamin and Barbara took some notes when Harry was talking, and they seemed interested in what he had to say. Barbara had similar ideas as to what the root cause was for the production decline; she had reached the conclusion that the company had not set aside an adequate budget for the production needs of the company. This was right in line with Harry's identified actionable problem of "restrictive financial practices."

Then the attention turned to Benjamin. He had thought about the problem differently than Harry and Barbara, and had reached the conclusion that the decline was because the production workers themselves were undervalued in the company. This was his root cause. The actionable problem he identified within his sphere of influence was low worker compensation, specifically a lack of a strong productivity-based bonus system. This was a shocking conclusion to Harry, but after seeing Benjamin's piece of paper with the root cause analysis exercise showing all of the logical steps, it became clear.

I know for certain that I would never have thought of this, but it makes sense, realized Harry, as he uncapped his pen and decided to steal Benjamin's idea.

"Fantastic work so far everyone. Now it is time to switch groups, so I want you all to find two new people you have not spoken with and form a group with them. This time you will get a bit more time, around twenty minutes. Go ahead."

Andrei Martins tapped Harry on the shoulder inviting him to form a group with him. Doris joined them, making a new group of three. This time around, Harry, Doris, and Andrei not only shared their own original ideas, but also what they had stolen from the first round of conversations. Harry really liked what Doris had to say and stole her idea, which was that the production decline was an innovation problem. She thought that because exploring new production techniques was not a priority, the company was suffering a decline. *Wow, she has spoken like true Research and Development leader*, thought Harry to himself as he excitedly stole her idea. Andrei and Harry also shared what they had stolen so far, and continued deep in conversation.

Pepe instructed everyone to form groups one last time for a final round of stealing. Harry now found himself with the always opinionated Lisa Zhu, and company President Mr. Yen. Although Harry might normally be intimidated asking for Mr. Yen's input, let alone 'steal' from him, Lisa broke the ice by jumping right in and excitedly sharing the ideas she has acquired and developed during the small group sessions.

"The production decline is simply a question of a lack of focus," Lisa confidently states. She continues, "I think that one reason output is slowing in the factories is because of outdated production machinery, which is a symptom of a lack of focus, or a lack of attention paid to the production process. Barbara from accounting helped me confirm this; she thought that the issue is because of a lack of appropriate budget for production…which comes back to my idea of a lack of focus. There is no appropriate budget because of the lack of focus!"

Mr. Yen and Harry nod at Lisa's comments. Harry may not have agreed completely with Lisa's ideas, but he was interested in how her original idea evolved and became stronger when she was tasked with stealing the ideas of others.

Then it was Mr. Yen's turn to share what he had been stealing. He was excited about what he had heard from Benjamin, which was that the production workers were not given the proper attention, both in terms of budget, but also in regards to appreciating their efforts and monitoring the conditions of the factory so that they may continue to work on a high level. Harry then shared with them what he had stolen so far, which was a combination of his original idea of conservative financial strategies and Doris's idea of a lack of innovation.

"Basically I think that the production decline is a result of the company being stuck with the old, traditional ways of doing things, and being overall too risk averse."

Mr. Yen nodded in thought when hearing this, and Lisa simply said "Wow."

Reaching Group Consensus

With the time given for stealing gone, Pepe continued the session by giving more instructions to the group. "Now that we have had our share of stealing, I want you all to stay in the groups you are in now. What you need to do as a group is to agree on the problems that would be worth solving. Argue if you need to, fight for what you think is best, but try to reach agreement in the end. It is important to narrow down the amount of problems we have agreed on, so just a few per group. You have ten minutes to do this and write them down as a group. When your group completes this task, have a member come to the front of the room and tape the paper up on the wall. Are there any questions? No? Alright, let's get started."

Everyone in the room jumped right into this activity, and intense conversation filled the air. As Harry, Mr. Yen, and Lisa discussed what they wanted to put down as the best idea, Harry realized that the three of them seemed to be on the same page, more or less. Harry concluded that restrictive financial practices were the core problem, and Lisa had a similar opinion, with her core problem being that the departmental budgets of the company were lacking focus. Mr. Yen did not change his tune about the lack of appreciation of production workers being a problem, and he thought they needed more recognition. He did concede that increased pay and an expanded bonus system for the workers was a budgetary issue as well, which allowed Mr. Yen, Lisa, and Harry all to agree that the core problem was budget related.

Upon reaching this conclusion, Harry wrote the words *Restrictive/unbalanced budgets* on his group's piece of paper and took it to the front of the room to tape it on the wall. As he did this, he took a moment to look at what the other groups had come up with: *lack of innovation, under motivated production workers/underfunded production department, no opportunity to propose change or new methods,* and *risk averse business practices.*

Interesting, all of us seem to have produced variants on the themes of innovation and budget, thought Harry. *I guess that makes sense considering the amount of stealing that was going on.*

Seeing that all the groups had agreed on a best ideas and then taped them to the wall, Pepe called everyone back together.

"Now let's read the ideas on the wall. Do we need to explain any of them?"

Everyone seemed to understand the ideas. Pepe's invitation for questions went unanswered so he continued on.

"There is one more step to complete. We are going to prioritize by writing our names next to the most important problems that you personally would like to solve. You may sign your name next to as many problems as you like, but be careful because signing your name next to a problem means that you are willing to work with others on a project or in a task force to actually try and solve the problem."

Most people signed their names next to *lack of innovation* and *underfunded production department.*

"It looks like we all more or less agree on the core problem which is behind this production decline." Does anyone have any questions or comments based on what we see written on the wall?

Voices filled the room as the group talked about how Soundless Component's lack of innovation and tendency to stick with their traditional ways have hurt the company. An understanding had been reached on what the real problem was, and because of this understanding, the Soundless Components employees were all on the same page as they began to talk about solutions and a plan on how to go forward. Harry could not believe what all that had been achieved in just a few hours.

Analysis: What Happened?

As far as I know, Harry Cheung, Lisa Zhu, and Soundless Components do not exist. I apologize if you are looking to purchase soundless headphone equipment. But what happened in the above example is real, and over the course of my career as a facilitator I have seen situations play out like the one above hundreds of times.

Before we can look at how Idealogue was used, we need to account for the context; what was the situation and what did we hope to accomplish? Soundless Components was calling an emergency meeting to address a company-wide problem. They were experiencing a production decline, and wanted to know what was causing this, and what they should do. The surface layer of the problem was there for all to see: a production decline. But what about the causes behind this problem? A lot of the time if a company is experiencing a crises or unexpected problem, it can be difficult for individuals to step back and see the entirety of the situation. Let us return for a moment to ice cream.

As you may remember, Sunday is the day when I eat ice cream for breakfast with my children. Our favorite flavor by far is blueberry. Every Sunday, rain or shine, it is blueberry ice cream for breakfast. I love this time because it is a nice bonding moment for us. I wish I could say the same for my kids, but I suspect that they love it not for the emotional closeness, but purely for the sugary blueberry ice cream. Anyhow, imagine for a moment that overnight, all the blueberries in the world have disappeared. My kids and I do not know this, and when I go to the store to get ice cream, there is no blueberry ice cream to buy! When I return home, my children already have their spoons and bowls ready, but instead I begin making pancakes. Although tasty, pancakes are not as good as blueberry ice cream, so my children begin to cry. I feel like crying too, as I hate to see them upset. I don't want my children crying and they don't want my pancakes. These things are often viewed as the main problem with a situation, but they are just unwanted results stemming from a deeper, core problem. In root cause analysis these unwanted results are called undesirable effects (UDE's for short). Since my children and I both experience a different UDE, it makes problem solving more difficult, as the same situation is perceived differently by us because of our different UDEs.

But what is the cause behind my version of the problem, crying children, and their version of the problem, my pancakes? What can we do to begin to take action to eliminate the UDE's that we are experiencing? This is where root cause analysis can help.

Root cause analysis allows my children and me to go beyond our respective undesirable effects and look at the bigger picture. When my children and I move past our own UDE's we can find a common starting place to face the problem, and from this common starting point, solutions are much more likely to emerge.

The employees of Soundless components faced a similar situation. They naturally viewed the production decline problem through their specific lens of job responsibility and acquired experience. Doris, from Research and Development first thought it was a problem caused by a lack of innovation. Benjamin, a manager of one of the production plants, spends a lot of his time working directly with the production workers themselves, so naturally he thought the decline was a result of the workers being underappreciated.

I have seen this as a facilitator many times, and also lived it myself in my personal life. My perspective and experience leads to my own unique point of view about a problem or situation. To reach a common understanding in a group situation like the one concerning Soundless Components, Idealogue, which is a consensus building tool, is a good start and it was made even more effective by combining it with root cause analysis.

What Tools Were Used?

1. Start with the undesired effects and build the cause-and-effect chain downwards.
2. Add entities that cause effects.
3. Check the logic of connections.
4. Locate root causes (entities with outbound arrow only). If a root cause is responsible for over 70% of symptoms, that is the core problem.
5. Draw your sphere of influence.
6. Select one or more problems within your sphere of influence.

Figure 21: The six steps of building a current reality tree, a type of a root cause analysis.

Thinking back to the third chapter, we remember that the very first stage of Idealogue is the individual stage, where people write down their own ideas in silence. This always has to happen before any stealing or group collaboration can occur. But within this individual stage is a lot of room for flexibility. That is to say that there are *many* different ways that people can write down their ideas individually. It is the responsibility of a good facilitator to give the proper instruction and to choose the best tool to use depending on what the specific situation calls for.

During the individual stage of Idealogue in my session with Soundless Components, I chose to have people make a *current reality tree*, which is a form of root cause analysis. I chose to use root cause analysis to help give the Soundless Components employees insight as to what could be the contributing factors behind the production decline. While it is natural and quite common to approach a problem from your own unique perspective, root cause analysis helps give people a sense of the bigger picture. The *current reality tree* tool, introduced by Eliyahu Goldratt, a true legend in the field of business communication, is one of many techniques used in root cause analysis. Other tools like fishbone analysis and the five whys are used to achieve the same goals as the *current reality* tree. Root cause analysis causes people to ask the question "Why?", and requires them to think about a problem or undesired effect, like production decline, on a deeper level. By starting with a problem and then thinking about the reasons behind it, a broader sense of that problem and how it fits within the whole system appears.

Another advantage of using this tool is that it can sometimes lead to surprising conclusions. Like we saw with Soundless Components, the core problem behind an undesirable effect is often unanticipated.

- Goldratt lived from 1947 to 2011.
- A business management and communications theorist.
- Best known for introducing his theory of constraints, which looks to identify factors or barriers that prevent goal achievement.
- Within the theory of constraints is the aim of root cause analysis: identify core problems.
- Goldratt then introduced tools and methods help do this, like the current reality tree.
- Goldratt's ideas and legacy live on, being taught at the Goldratt institute, which he founded in 1986.
- Learn more about Goldwratt by reading some of his key texts:

The Goal: A Process of Ongoing Improvement (1984)
Critical Chain (2002)
What is this thing called Theory of Constraints? (1999)

Figure 22: A brief biography and some key texts of Eliyahu Goldratt.

Root Cause analysis is not a perfect tool, it does have its shortcomings. One of these shortcomings is that it is an individual tool at heart. Logic is not shared between people, and even if you and I reach the same conclusion to a problem, we might take very different roads in arriving there. Simply put, people have different implicit logic systems, and it can be quite a challenge understanding another person's logic. What seems like an obvious conclusion to them may seem like a departure from reality to me or you! This makes it a challenge to use root cause analysis in group settings as a standalone tool; you cannot easily create a 100% consensus on logic behind the problems, especially if you are working with a large group. That being said, it is a great tool that allows people to better understand a problem and generate ideas as to why a problem is occurring which is exactly what was needed for the problem solving session we visited with Soundless Components.

There is a small tool that absolutely has to be mentioned. The group prioritized the results by writing their names next to the problem that they wanted to help solve. You do not want to leave the group with the problems and no plan on solving them, and prioritizing with names helps you form groups or task forces for creating solutions to the problems. Prioritizing with names is very practical, easy to incorporate in a session, and one of my favorite methods.

Why Idealogue?

When I was working with the employees of Soundless Components, I made sure to structure the day around the five stages of Idealogue. Although I depended on root cause analysis to generate ideas, the session would not have been successful without Idealogue. The shortcomings of root cause analysis were nullified by the Idealogue stages of repeated conversations in small groups and the core of Idealogue; steal with pride. As mentioned, the current reality tree is often used as an individual tool, and it can be difficult using it with groups, as connections and cause-and-effect relationships that seem obvious to one person can sound like complete rubbish to another person. The good news is that Idealogue directly covers up the shortcomings of the current reality tree. By tasking people to find the very best ideas and by making them responsible for writing the best ideas down, they are required to not just listen to other ideas, but to understand them.

If Idealogue was absent from the session, fragmented viewpoints and insurmountable gaps between individual logic systems would most likely have been the result. It is like the story of two blind friends who take a trip to the Zoo together. They are shown around by a nice employee of the zoo, who takes them up to an animal. Since the men cannot see, the zoo employee allows them to go into an animal habitat, and feel an animal so that they can get acquainted with it. The first blind man touches the animal, and says that it is skinny and long, and he declares that it is a giant snake.

The second blind man touches the animal, and tells his friend that he is crazy. "This cannot possibly be a snake, it is big and round. I think that this isn't even an animal, but a tree!"

The Zoo worker says that both of them are wrong. What they are feeling is an elephant. Each blind man has his own idea about what they experienced, and their mind is made up. But what if they were to talk about how they arrived at their conclusion?

As I am sure you remember, Idealogue is named by combining the words "idea" and "dialogue". If the blind men were to share their experience and ideas and the logic behind them, they may have concluded that it was in fact an elephant.

The example of the blind men at the zoo is a good illustration of how the Soundless Components employees viewed the production decline problem before the problem solving meeting. They naturally viewed the production decline problem through their specific lens of job responsibility and acquired experience.

The first step of Idealogue invites people to write down their ideas individually, and for this we can use a number of different facilitative tools to help people do this to the best of their ability. The tools we choose do not even need to be great group-level tools either, as the remaining stages of Idealogue cancel out the shortcomings of the tool selected for idea generation. Soundless Components needed to find the reasons behind a production decline, and root cause analysis was an obvious choice to help achieve these aims. Using a current reality tree for the first individual idea stage of Idealogue is not the only option. Sometimes other tools may be better, or sometimes no tool at all is required beyond just instructing participants to write down their thoughts. If there are time constraints, or if people are arriving to the session with a high level of knowledge about the situation, or have worked with the problem or issue previously in a group setting, then sometimes the best way to proceed is to just allow a few minutes for the individual stage and then jump right into small group formation and the stealing of ideas. It is the facilitator's responsibility to select the best tool for the situation.

Later on when people begin stealing with pride, ideas (and the logic systems driving these ideas) build on each other, with the end result being a new idea or insight that could not have been possible by using individual level tools. But when used together, they strengthen each other: root cause analysis acts as the muscle and the stages of Idealogue act as the skeleton. When people are placed into the first small group to steal, individual ideas combine and new knowledge is produced. When these people then form other small groups for additional rounds of stealing, these ideas are further spread and developed and transformed into group consensus.

Chapter 6
Deployment Meeting

It was a typical autumn day on the Baltic Sea; windy, grey, and a bit cold. I was aboard a large ship called the Baltic Breeze, headed from Helsinki to Stockholm. As I sipped a large cup of coffee, I realized that I was doing something that was quite strange for me; I was looking at a catalog that advertised hockey clothing and accessories. A lot of people from Scandinavia are crazy about hockey. They drink and shout with happiness when their team wins, and if their team loses, well, then they also drink but this time they shout with anger and sadness. I am not one of these people. Frankly, I couldn't care less about hockey. The reason I was looking at this catalog selling hockey jerseys, hockey pucks, hockey skates, and hockey hats was because I was on my way to facilitate a deployment session with a large Swedish labor union called HAM. No, this time HAM does not refer to a type of sandwich, but rather the Hockey Apparel Manufacturers labor union of Sweden.

I usually do facilitation sessions and workshops for private companies, but when I work in Sweden it is common for me to run sessions for labor unions. In Sweden, there is a rich history of labor unions, and almost all employees that work in either manufacturing or in the public sector belong to a union of some sort. This is fantastic for the employees as the unions are great advocates of employee rights by making sure that employees are treated fairly, and paid properly. They are taken quite seriously in Sweden.

HAM is no exception, and since hockey is the national pastime of Sweden HAM has thousands of members. Ham is like a big family, and it is self-sustaining, meaning that member dues pay for all the costs that are required to run and maintain the union. Like many labor unions, all of the services and needs that HAM requires are provided in house. I knew that most labor unions are like big families, and they can be fiercely protective of their own. *HAM may be even more protective than most unions* I thought to myself as I remembered who was serving as the Union Leader, a guy simply known as "the iron man."

The iron man worked in a plant that produced hockey pucks. His real name was Magnus Axelsson, and he was a promising hockey player himself in his youth. He loved the game so much that he decided to have a career in hockey no matter what, so when he realized that he could not become a professional hockey player he got a job in a hockey equipment manufacturing plant. Legend had it that he had the chance for a promotion, but instead stayed in the grueling entry level job of lifting barrel after barrel of melted hot rubber, which was needed to make hockey pucks. He was a no-nonsense, tough man, but he was beloved among the union because he was fair, and he loved to go to battle on behalf of union members.

The reason I was getting involved with HAM was because of a recent decision made by the Iron Man and a few other top union officials that will impact the entire labor union. I was here to help a group of around 50 union officials receive the news, understand it, and talk to the Iron Man about it. The decision had been made, and now it just needed to be deployed to the group, hence this type of meeting was called a "deployment meeting."

As I saw the city of Stockholm come into view as the boat prepared for port, I hoped that my lack of enthusiasm for Hockey would not be a problem during my time working with HAM; I did not want any problems between me and the Iron Man.

The Session Begins

The next morning I was standing in a nice conference room in downtown Stockholm. Sitting in front of me were about 50 union representatives; each person an elected official there to represent his or her own district. In the front row I saw the Iron Man. *Jeez, I guess the nickname really fits this guy*, I thought as I politely nodded at the musclebound, 2 meter tall man. He returned my greeting, but never took off the stern, concerned look on his face. I could tell that he was a bit nervous for today's meeting, and he was probably very worried about how the group would receive the news he was about to break to them.

It was time for the session to begin so I greeted the room full of HAM members and thanked them for inviting me to Stockholm.

"I must admit I am not the most knowledgeable about hockey, so I hope that after the session maybe all of you can teach me a thing or two. Speaking of knowledge, I want to talk for a moment about why we are here in this meeting today. The objective for this meeting is to create understanding about the organizational changes concerning the IT department".

After I had introduced the meeting itinerary and the format of how we as a group would be working, the Iron Man sttod up and begin to explain, but I cut him short.

"It is not quite yet time for you to begin your presentation yet. I want everyone in the audience to take a moment to get into small groups of three or four and discuss why we are here. Everyone has about four minutes to do this, so please begin."

The audience reacted well to my instructions, and everyone began chatting in small groups. I knew that most people did not know the details of what changes the Iron Man was about to announce, but that didn't matter. I just wanted people to begin the day by talking and waking up a bit. The audience knew that they were here to discuss something big, otherwise they would not have been asked to come and meet in Stockholm. After the four minutes were up I asked for a few volunteers to share what they had discussed in groups.

A hand went up from the back of the room and a voice said, "I think we are here to discuss some bad news. See how nervous the Iron Man looks? The last time I have seen him like this he had to announce the reduction of Union benefits!"

Someone else called out, "No, you are wrong. The news is big, but it is nothing bad." The original volunteer replied, "Then what is that hockey hater from Finland doing here? Why would we have outside help if it were something good?"

I, the hockey hater from Finland, replied, "Thanks for your ideas everyone, but I will let all of you decide for yourselves if it is good or bad. I took this opportunity to introduce my questions which I had posted on the wall. "After the presentation I am going to ask you to think on your own about the following questions; what are the key points of the presentation you just heard? Next, what is your immediate reaction to the presentation? And finally, after hearing the presentation, what questions do you have for your leader Magnus? Your answers will be shared in small groups".

"We are here to discuss a bit of news and who better to present this news than your leader himself, Magnus Axelsson." When Magnus was introduced, he stood up and walked to the front of the room. The audience clapped and a few even began cheering him on by calling out, "Iron Man! Iron Man!"

The Iron Man was a good leader, but he was not charismatic in the traditional sense. He had no patience for small talk or social niceties. He was a man of few words, and he liked to get straight to the point. Today was no exception and his presentation was as direct as can be.

"We are here today to announce a big change within HAM. Our I.T. team that has been based in Stockholm has been outsourced. They will be absorbed by the company EuroTech, and EuroTech will now be providing all of our technological needs. The I.T. employees have the choice to continue working with HAM by moving to Glasgow to work in the EuroTech offices, or they can resign and accept compensation. Among the IT team, 18 people have decided to move to Glasgow, and 2 will be accepting compensation and resigning. This is effective immediately. This decision is based on efficiency, and it will help HAM grow in the future. HAM is growing, and in order for our I.T. team to meet our needs they needed more resources; new servers, more employees, and better equipment. These needs would cost HAM too much, so outsourcing them to a company that can provide these needs like EuroTech is a logical choice."

The audience was relatively quiet during the presentation, and after the Iron Man had finished there was a second or two of stunned silence before the audience erupted.

"You can't do this, we are a union, we do not act like pigs!"

"HAM is falling apart!"

"Is this even legal?!"

I motioned for the Iron Man to sit back down as I tried to take back control of the room.

"First of all, thank you Magnus for the presentation. I know that this is a big change, and I assure you that all of your questions will be answered. That is why we are here today, and to do this as effectively as possible I would like everyone to please quiet down and hold off on your questions for a moment."

The chatter died down a bit, so I continued to give instructions.

1. What are the key points of the presentation you just heard?
2. What is your immediate reaction to the presentation?
3. What questions do you have for Magnus?

Figure 23: The questions Pepe gave to HAM before the presentation.

"First I want everyone to take out a piece of paper and something to write with. You all have five minutes to think about the presentation you just heard, and write down your thoughts. You are going to do this by writing down your answers to the three questions I gave you about the presentation. Take your time, and please, no talking."

Everyone began writing intensely. The atmosphere in the room was charged and serious, and many people seemed to have taken the Iron Man's presentation personally. As everyone wrote, I could see that the Iron Man looked worried, and even a bit sick.

"Magnus, how are you feeling?", I whispered.

In his no-nonsense style, Magnus replied, "Not good."

"That's OK, but just give it some time. People need a few moments to process the news and figure out for themselves what it means. I think that by the end of the session the atmosphere will be much more positive and you will be feeling better."

I left Magnus to his thoughts as I began setting up the room for the next stage of the session. While the group was finishing writing down their responses to the three questions I gave them, I walked around the room and placed large pieces of paper and a marker in different places. Once I had finished this, the time given for the individual stage had expired and I instructed the participants to form groups of three and to start stealing ideas. "In your groups I want you to talk about the three questions you just wrote about. If you hear someone else say something that makes sense, steal it for yourself by writing it down. Discuss your answers and do not be afraid to defend your answers or question other people's answers. You have ten minutes to do this."

Forming New Groups by Fleeing Sharks

"We are going to change the groups, I have an interesting method for forming new groups. It is called the Shark and it takes 3 minutes. Is it ok if we try it?" There was a long silence and finally Ulla, Magnus's talkative secretary, said, "Pepe, the Shark sounds interesting, let's give it a try."

"OK everyone. Now take the paper you have been writing on and stand up. We are going to form small groups, but in a unique way. Can everyone please walk to the front of the room towards Magnus and me?"

Chairs scraped and papers rustled as 50 or so people stood up and came to the front of the room.

"Do any of you enjoy swimming?" I asked the group.

"I like it, but only in a heated pool," someone replied.

"Not me, I only like frozen water. You need *ice* to play hockey, which is what I like to do."

"I jump in the sea once or twice a year. It is cold, but very invigorating." Someone tried to respond to this by beginning to say how crazy it was to swim in the cold water of the Baltic, but I cut them off and continued.

"Thanks for the replies everyone. I love swimming myself. But I am deathly afraid of sharks. We are going to form small groups to work in right now, but we are going to do it by playing a game. I want all of you to go for a *swim* by walking around the room. Enjoy it, relax, and have fun. But swimming is dangerous because unfortunately there are sharks. So when I see a shark, I will shout a number. You will be safe if you will form an island with that number of participants. Ready?

People began 'swimming' around the room. I let everyone have time to mix up and spread around the room before I gave the loud warning, "Three!"

People jumped around, looking to form islands of three. I must say I was a bit surprised by their competitiveness. I even saw the serious Iron Man lunge to find an island, a determined look on his face. *It must be a hockey thing* I thought.

When everyone had found sanctuary on an island, I continued.

"Great job! No shark victims yet. That alone makes for a good day. Look around at the other people sharing your island with you. These people are your group-mates. In your groups I want you to steal ideas and write the best ideas on your own piece of paper. If there is a fact that you did not capture yet, a first reaction that well describes your feeling, or a question that really gets to the point, please write it down. You have fifteen minutes to do this."

I walked around different islands, I mean groups, and listened to bits and pieces of different discussions. One group was debating what the presentation was about, and two people were arguing if it was relevant that most of the I.T. team had decided to accept the outsourcing and move to Glasgow.

Another group was fired up, and all three people in that group were questioning out loud how such a decision could even be made without all of the thousands of HAM members voting on it.

"-and I don't even think that Iron Man can make this decision alone. He is our leader but-"

"We don't know how he made the decision. Actually, we should ask him that. Write that question down."

With the ten minutes gone, I had everyone stand up, and come to the front of the room again. We had entered the repeated group formation stage of Idealogue, so people needed to find new people to talk with. I told everyone that it was time for them to go for another swim, and I repeated the shark method to get them into new groups.

"When you hear the shark warning, this time you can't form an island that has a person from your old island on it. So new islands and new people to talk with. Discuss the same three questions and steal good ideas from others. After another twelve minutes of discussion, you will have eight minutes to summarize your conversation and write on the flipchart that I will give to your group."

People swam and I gave the shark warning, forcing people into new groups. Everyone discussed some more, and after twelve minutes, I let the group know what was going to happen next.

"Now that all of you have had a chance to talk about things a bit, I want each group to summarize what you talked about on the big piece of paper that is on the wall. Write largely enough so that others can read what it says because these papers will be presented later on. You have eight minutes to summarize your group conversation. If there are no questions you can start now."

Each group began putting their thoughts and conversations down onto the large pieces of paper. Each group was doing this slightly differently; some were writing in complete sentences and in paragraphs, others were using a bullet point system, and I even saw one group begin to draw large pictures on their paper. All of this was OK. The last thing they needed were restrictions on how they could express themselves at this point. It was more important for everyone to feel unrestricted and be able to summarize their conversations however they wanted.

With the help of a few volunteers, I collected all of the flipcharts, and taped them to the wall at the front of the room.

Summarizing to Make Things Clear

"Fantastic work everyone! Now I want all of you to look at the flipcharts. If you don't understand what something means, ask. And if you have the answer to someone else's question, feel free to help them out and reply."

Everyone crowded around the flipcharts and began reading and asking questions. The Iron Man had a question almost immediately.

"Why is there a drawing of a building on fire on this paper?"

Some people laughed and crowded around him to see what he was looking at.

A woman answered him, "that's not a building on fire, it is a burning computer. I drew it to capture our group's feeling of doubt about how well our system will work with the outsourced I.T. team."

The Iron Man nodded, now understanding what it meant. The group continued on asking and answering each other's questions. Some of the questions revolved around bad handwriting, or pointing out that a word was misspelled. The content of the flip charts was rather similar, reflecting the gradual building of consensus and understanding that happened during the small group stages.

The questions died down, and I gave the group their next task.

"On this wall we have 16 pieces of paper; the summarized thoughts of what all of you had to say when talking with others about today's presentation. Now I would like you to discuss in your groups of three how all of these papers can be summarized."

After six minutes I asked, "Who is brave enough to try and go first?"

A middle-aged man stepped forward. He glanced at all of the papers hanging on the wall, and began.

"The facts are clear. The IT department is moving to Glasgow. The emotional climate is more interesting. Actually, most of the people think the decision is rational and acceptable. However, people are worried about service quality and they are sad about losing their old friends. Also, some people are afraid that out-sourcing will become a common policy of HAM. Then the papers go on to list a few questions that we all have. Most of the questions are small technical things like 'what number do we call when we have a technical emergency?' A few questions are more wide reaching, for example this one, 'does it violate union policy for a decision like this to be made without a union-wide vote?' "

The volunteer was finished summarizing, so I thanked him. People seemed to have a much better understanding of the new change, and a lot of their questions had been answered by other participants during the idea-stealing phase.

The Iron Man Explains Things Further

There still was one last phase of the meeting; a question and answer session. I asked Magnus to come to the front of the room, and I told everyone that now was the time to ask any questions that have not already been answered.

Magnus looked at the questions on the papers and began: "Are we safe was one of your worries. Outsourcing the I.T. department was not a decision taken lightly, and it is not a decision that we would normally make. To answer your question, yes, you all are safe. The I.T. department did a great job for us, but the expenses of keeping them in house and working privately for us were too much. No other departments cost the union nearly as much as they did, so it is unlikely we would ever find the need to outsource anyone else. Most jobs are not able to be outsourced anyway.

Another popular question is about how this decision was made, and many people thought we should have gone to a vote when the issue is a big one like this. The I.T. department works for us, the hockey apparel manufacturers. It is an important for all of you to know that your voices are listened to and appreciated, but this issue is really a procedural one and does not require a vote. We are not deciding together about going on a strike, or endorsing another union or some political measure. Instead this is an administrative decision about making HAM run as efficiently as possible. And as your leader it is my job to make these decisions to the best of my ability. And no one on the I.T. team resents this choice as far as I know. Being outsourced allows them to join a company that specializes in their field, and they will be able to grow professionally. And those who do not want to move to Glasgow and join EuroTech are being compensated for their trouble. As far as I know, there is no resentment on their side."

The crowd was reacting positively to what the Iron Man had to say, but another important question was called out; "before, we had an I.T. person available in office. When something went wrong, we could just find them and talk to them physically. How does this work now?"

"That's a good question, and I do not know the answer now, but I am sure we will find a good alternative easily enough. Procedural and technical questions are great, but they are not the best type of questions to ask right now. We have all your questions recorded now and each one of them will be addressed as soon as possible."

Magnus did a fine job answering all the questions he could and I continued:

"To end today I want to thank you for such a good session and I want to congratulate all of you on what was achieved today. Is it fair to say that everyone feels much more comfortable about the change that was announced today?"

The group agreed, and I even saw the Iron Man nodding and maybe even smiling a little bit too.

The session concluded and everyone filed out, with some people asking me questions about how I liked Sweden, and if I had a favorite Swedish hockey team. I answered the question as best I could by saying that I enjoyed myself every time I had the chance to travel to Sweden, and that despite becoming friendly with the members of HAM, I still held absolutely zero interest in hockey.

1. Beginning
   - Introduction and the schedule for the day
   - Small-group discussion
2. Presentation
   - The questions were introduced
   - Presentation of the facts
3. Idealogue
   - Individual stage
   - Rotating groups of three discussing and stealing answers
   - Groups of three summarizing
   - Small groups summarized the work of all groups
4. Answers and thank you
   - The presenter answered remaining questions
   - Thank you!

Figure 24: The stages of the deployment meeting.

Analysis: What Happened Here?

Normally Idealogue is used in sessions to help a group reach consensus about an issue by discussing it and then defining it together as a group. Remember Assorted Nigeria Limited working together to decide the future vision of their company? How about Soundless components identifying the cause of their problems as a team?

This is not possible if a boss or someone higher up has already made the decision, so in deployment meetings (also called change kick-off meetings or workshops) first a presentation is given to the group which explains the decision and what will happen within the company. This is an important change because now the workshop needs to help people understand and come to terms with a decision that is based on the logic of another person, as opposed to the previous examples we have seen where a group comes up with ideas and reaches consensus together about what ideas are logical. This means that we have to create an atmosphere where the change is justified.

1. **Unfreeze**

2. **Change**

3. **Refreeze**

Figure 25: Kurt Lewin's change model.

When I was working with HAM, the group did not first understand that there were problems with keeping the I.T. department in house and *then* decide to outsource them, but they needed to be helped along to understand that the change was needed and then they their attitudes needed to be shaped so that they would accept the change. This situation is a textbook example from Kurt Lewin's Change Management Model. Lewin was one of the giants in the field of psychology, and in his life (1890-1947) he developed many influential tools. His change management model explains what needs to happen in order for an organization to successfully adopt change, and the model explains all this by using ice as an analogy.

Pretend that you are throwing yourself a birthday party. You are a great person, and you think you deserve a proper celebration. At your party you want to have cold drinks that are served over ice. But normal ice simply will not do for you. You are going to make ice cubes into the shape of stars to represent just how great you and your party are. So what do you need to do in order to make this happen? You first need to take your normal ice and unfreeze it. Then you are going to mold it (change it) to your desired shape of stars, and finally you are going to re-freeze it. This process for your birthday is the same as Lewin's model for organizational change. The model is divided into three phases; unfreeze, change, and re-freeze.

During the unfreeze stage, the current thoughts and attitudes held by people within the organization are questioned, and new alternatives are presented to the group. This gets people to realize that there are other ways of doing things, and that they do not need stay stuck in their current ways. Here it is important to help people understand the change and to deal with their emotions.

Next is the change stage. At this point the change is implemented and the old ways are abandoned. Lewin's model ends with the re-freeze stage. At this point people are experiencing the results of the change, and seeing firsthand how it affects them. Any small problems or difficulties should be talked about and resolved.

The deployment meeting we saw with the HAM labor union was held to help people get through the unfreeze stage. The new details were presented to the group, and people were able to begin the process of coming to terms with the change.

Many of us thrive on predicable routines and structure. This makes us feel safe. When change is introduced we feel very uncomfortable, so it is important to give us a chance to talk about our feelings and to get acquainted with the facts.

What Tools Were Used and Why?

After warming up the group by asking them to talk to each other about why they thought they were having the meeting, I gave the floor to Magnus "the Iron Man" Axelsson so that he could present the change to them. His presentation was the key bit of information that the group would discuss during Idealogue. I asked them to think about the presentation with three things in mind:

1. What were the key facts/important parts of the presentation?
2. What is your first reaction to the presentation?
3. What questions do you have for Magnus after hearing his presentation?

The first question about the key facts forces people to put the presentation into their own words as they attempt to summarize it. When they share these key facts in the group stages of Idealogue, a group consensus of what the presentation was about will emerge, and people will answer each other's questions. The presentation or implemented change may seem quite clear to the "big boss" who came up with it, but people always understand things differently, so group level comprehension cannot be taken for granted. This means that it is an important step of deployment meetings to have people recap the key facts of the presentation to themselves and then to share these key fact with others.

The second question about a person's first reaction to the news is important because it allows people to write down their emotional response to the presentation. Sharing these emotions in groups during Idealogue is a type of therapy which quickly helps the group come to terms with rather big changes or decisions. People are actually unaware of their feelings and their complexity. Hearing other people's feelings and discussing them helps identify and justify your own emotions. Identifying your emotions will help you deal with them.

The third question asks people to write down the questions that they have for the boss. The key function of the meeting is to help people understand the change. Writing down questions makes sure that all doubts are documented and will be responded to, and that nothing important was left uncovered.

Watch Out! SHARK!

As you may have noticed during my time with HAM, it was a tense session. Some people were not happy at first about the I.T. team being outsourced, and the Iron Man was also nervous when he had to give the news to the group. I tried to ease the tension by using the shark group formation method. I needed to put people into groups anyway, so why not make a game out of it? It can sometimes feel awkward asking a group of adults to pretend to swim around desks and then flee from imaginary sharks, but I usually see positive reactions from people when I use this formation method. It lightens the mood, and accomplishes an objective that needs to be achieved at the same time.

1. Participants walk freely around.
2. The Facilitator shouts a number. Participants have to form islands with that number of people.
3. The slow ones who did not fit into the islands will be eaten by the sharks (but you still let them continue).
4. After a few rounds the facilitator shouts the ideal number for the next exercise, which prompts people to form new groups.

Shark is an energising tool for dividing a large group into sub-groups.

Figure 26: The Shark group formation method.

Feedback by Summarizing and a Final Q & A Session.

At the end of the session I made sure to have everyone summarize what had been discussed by reading the notes on the flipcharts that were created in small groups. This was a way for the group to create a shared understanding. It was also a way for me to get feedback and understand how well the session went. As a facilitator I need to know if everyone got the message or if there were lots of negative emotions. If the group still hated the change, then I would know that more work needed to be done and the presented change needed to be talked about more.

The last part of the deployment session was a final question and answer session where Magnus answered the questions listed on the flipcharts. This was a final opportunity to clear up any doubts or have something explained further. The final question and answer session serves as a transitioning point from the unfreeze stage of Lewin's model to the change stage.

Why Idealogue?

In the final chapter about planning workshops, I will tell you that Idealogue is a bad method for situations where a group has to address multiple questions. But in this session with HAM, I used Idealogue with three different questions. How is this possible? Idealogue works with many questions when they are related and consequential. First you experience information (facts), and then immediately afterwards you experience a feeling about the information. Finally, if something remains unclear, you have questions about the topic. The three questions also apply to every single person in the room equally. Everyone can summarize what they just heard, everyone has a reaction to it, and everyone can decide if they have more questions after hearing the presentation.

Idealogue also helps people internalize the message of the presentation and remember it. This is done by repetition. First the message is presented by the boss. Then people think about it and summarize it for themselves during the individual stage. Next come three rounds of sharing and stealing in small groups, followed by their flipcharts being displayed at the front of the room and summarized yet again! That means that under the structure of Idealogue, the message of the presentation is repeated six different times! This is very important because even if a presentation seems straightforward with little room for interpretation, it still can be understood differently by different people. A lot of the time people hear what they want to hear. By repeating the message again and again using Idealogue, you are helping to build shared understanding and agreement in the group about what the presentation really meant. Using Idealogue also regulates any questions that the group has. Instead of having hundreds and hundreds of questions for the boss, people answer each other's questions, leaving only the biggest and most common questions for the boss to reply to at the end of the session.

One important reason for using Idealogue during deployment meetings or workshops is that it is therapeutic. As you know, change can be hard for some people and if you suddenly remove the status-quo and predictability from working life, people can be initially upset or angry. Idealogue gets people talking about their emotions in groups, and in this case asking people what their first reaction was to the presentation is the same as asking, "How do you feel about all of this?" It creates the opportunity for people to get everything off of their chest and out into the open in a constructive way.

Chapter 7
Creativity

Peter's Problem

Peter Smudge could feel himself grinding his teeth. He knew that this was simply a stress reaction and that he was just reacting to the current situation he found himself in. Peter tried to ignore that symptom and focus on the task at hand. He looked at the lone piece of paper sitting in front of him on his desk. Peter was a man married to routine, and when he was taking notes, writing emails, or keeping a journal, he always labeled each page with a heading, and today was no exception. At the top upper right, in his neat penmanship, was the date, location, and event name.

Peter Smudge
September 17th, 2015.
Creativity Session with facilitator P. Nummi

Peter went on grinding his teeth and continued staring at his paper. He was having a difficult time. You see, Peter Smudge, a man of routine, order, and predictability, was lacking all of those things on this day. The reason? He was participating in a creativity session with facilitator Pepe Nummi.

Pepe was asked by Peter's employer, Darn Good Donuts (known as DGD for short) to come and lead the entire staff of the company headquarters in a session designed to create new, innovative ideas. Sitting in the meeting room with the other 32 HQ employees of DGD was not the problem for Peter. The problem for Peter was the first activity that Pepe had assigned to the group. Peter thought back on the instructions Pepe gave to the group.

"You have all seen one of these, isn't that right?" asked Pepe, while holding up a blank piece of computer paper. The entire group nodded the affirmative and Pepe continued. "What is the common use for a piece of paper?"

Peter knew the answer so he said, "A piece of paper can be used to capture impressions during the writing or printing process."

"Thanks Peter, that was quite the clinical and scientific definition. What I want all of you to do now is to find other uses for this piece of paper. The instructions for this activity are simple. Take two minutes and write down all the things you can think of that can be done with a piece of paper. The time starts....NOW!"

At the word 'NOW', Peter's coworkers began writing. Some people seemed to have dozens of ideas, while others wrote down things at a more measured pace, but everyone seemed to have a steady stream of ideas nonetheless. Unfortunately for Peter, things were going a bit more slowly and after forty seconds, he only had one lonely idea written down:

A piece of paper can be used to capture impressions during the writing or printing process.

As the seconds kept ticking by, Peter began to feel just a tiny bit sorry for himself, and about how such a task did not apply to him. *I'm not cut out for this and despite that, I have already given the group a sound, detailed definition of what a piece of paper is used for…to ask anything more is just excessive and silly. I have no need for creativity in my job, I am not that creative anyways…and that's what makes me so effective in my work as head of the Franchisee Regulatory Adherence Committee.*

As the head of the Franchisee Regulatory Adherence Committee, it fell on Peter's shoulders to ensure that each of the DGD donut store franchises complied with the 45 page manual of regulations that Peter himself helped draw up. Peter felt his job was very black and white. He spent his days checking in on stores to make sure that, among other things, they have the correct inventory of ingredients, and that the DGD house blend coffee was served at precisely the optimum donut-dipping temperature of 172 degrees Fahrenheit. Peter even viewed his job as making sure none of the store owners were getting creative on their own and trying to depart from the manual of regulations which Peter viewed as a sacred text for success.

Even with these beliefs in Peter's mind, he still could see how today's meeting was important to him. The meeting was a session intended to create ideas for new products and franchising opportunities for DGD.

Just as Peter was getting especially down on himself for not being able to think of any creative uses for a piece of paper, a drop of DGD dark roast coffee fell from his mug as he was taking a sip.

Peter watched as the drop of coffee landed onto his piece of paper and was absorbed.

Inspiration struck, and Peter had a second idea to add to his paper:

A piece of paper can be used to absorb spilled coffee in the absence of napkins.

"OK everyone, another 30 seconds and then time's up!", called out Pepe.

The rapid approaching deadline inspired Peter to also write down two more ideas, based on the other liquids that Peter had consumed that day:

A piece of paper can be used to absorb spilled milk in the absence of napkins.

A piece of paper can be used to absorb spilled water in the absence of napkins.

Peter, and the other 31 DGD employees put down their pencils and pens as Pepe called an end to the allowed time.

"So, was everyone able to write down at least a few ideas?" The whole group, even Peter, nodded as Pepe went on. "Let's hear a bit of what you all came up with," Pepe said while scanning the room.

Tameka Taylor, head of supplier relations, held up a small paper swan and answered first. "You can make origami, like this one."

Peter cursed himself for not relying on his knowledge of Japanese handicrafts, while the rest of the room admired Tameka's handiwork.

"You can play football!" offered Lizzy, the systems administrator for the DGD webpage as she crumpled up a piece of paper into a ball, dropped it on the ground and gave it a kick.

"And basketball too!", yelled Lorn, the CFO of DGD. Lorn was a bit over enthusiastic in his attempts to demonstrate his idea, and nearly hit Pepe in the head with his piece of paper.

"You know I was aiming for the trash can Pepe….sorry."

Pepe however was not bothered in the least. "No problem at all, I am shocked by the enthusiasm and creativity shown by all of you. A lot of the time when I use this activity with a group, people have real trouble thinking of more than just one or two ideas. Good job everyone. "

Hearing this, Peter looked down at ideas neatly listed on his piece of paper, and felt a bit better. *Pepe said that some people think of even fewer ideas than three, so I can't feel too bad.*

Peter realized that he absolutely cannot feel bad at all regarding his ideas when he heard what Pepe had to say next.

"I want all of you to think about the people I mentioned that have a hard time thinking of creative ideas. What do you think their biggest challenge is?"

"A lack of confidence," guessed Jack, who was the head of virtual advertising.

"Basically yes. I think the main problem that limits creativity is self-criticism. Any idea is a good idea, especially in a session like today's where the goal is to generate new ideas. Do not be afraid to limit yourself by judging your own ideas. I want all of you to take a look at your pieces of paper with the ideas written on them. Can someone tell me the very first idea for the use of a piece of paper that they came up with?"

A hand went up, volunteering. The hand belonged to Sylvia Smyth, the CEO of the company. "My first idea was to make a paper airplane."

"Thank you. Someone else?"

Peter volunteered and shared his first idea, that paper could be used for writing or printing purposes.

Pepe thanked Peter and asked for one more example of someone's first idea for the use of a piece of paper.

"One piece of paper can be attached to a bunch of others to make a magazine or a book," replied Joanna, who was the head secretary and logistics coordinator of the company.

"Thanks Joanna. So we have heard three examples of the first idea that came to mind; make a paper airplane, write on it, and make books. My question for you is this. Are these ideas new to you or are they things you have done or seen before?"

The DGD employees sat, pondering Pepe's question. The answer was quickly becoming obvious as Pepe went on:

"I think we can all agree that these ideas come from memory. We all have read books, and as children we have probably made and thrown paper airplanes. Peter gave us the core use for paper in his first idea, by saying that it can be used for writing or printing. When we are trying to think of ideas, often times the first ones that come to mind are based from memory. In fact, a creativity guru named Edward de Bono claimed that there are three levels of thinking; first the natural thinking that is based on memory, then the logical thinking that is a logical extension of what is known and finally the lateral thinking which is based on creativity[6]. We usually think in the first two levels and it can be a challenge to go on to the creative level. Many of the ideas that come from the logic and memory levels are great, but we also need to try and reach the creative level because it is in the creative level where new, outside of the box ideas are born."

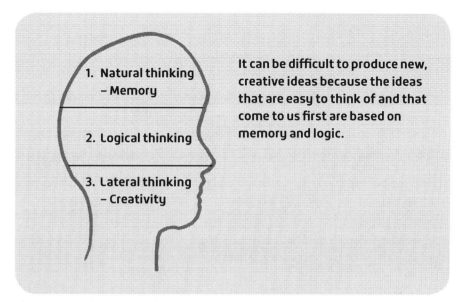

1. Natural thinking
   – Memory

2. Logical thinking

3. Lateral thinking
   – Creativity

It can be difficult to produce new, creative ideas because the ideas that are easy to think of and that come to us first are based on memory and logic.

Figure 27: The three levels of thinking as outlined by Edward de Bono.

Peter was impressed to see the creative process mapped out and explained by using the three levels of thinking, and he began to feel a bit better about the creativity session and what he could potentially offer to it. *Maybe I'm not the only one who has problems leaving memory and logic behind. I saw a few other people nod in agreement when Pepe talked about being stuck in the first two levels... now that I know this, I think it will be easier for me to come up with creative ideas!*

Peter's new found optimism would be put to the test immediately though, as Pepe had another task for the group.

---

[6] Actually De Bono also talks about mathematical thinking that is based on rules for processing information. The author – due to his lack of deeper understanding – has just considered mathematical thinking a type of logical thinking and ignored the category.

Lateral Thinking

"Can someone please tell me a type of animal that you think is interesting?" After a brief pause, the replies came in quickly, being shouted at once by several different people.

"A fox!"

"A zebra."

"My cat Whiskers!"

The group chuckled and Pepe proceeded. "Very good, thank you. I think we will use the fox as an example. Can you all tell me some characteristics of the fox? What makes the fox interesting?"

"I know that they have water-resistant fur and can live in either the heat or the snow," said Aldo, who was the person to give the fox as an example of an interesting animal."

"Thank you Aldo. What else?" asked Pepe to the group.

Joanna added, "I know that foxes are adaptable and can thrive in a lot of places. I see them in the city park near my house sometimes."

And in came a third reply from Lorn; "they are bright red and nice to look at."

"Thanks everyone. Now we are going to return to thinking about paper once more, but this time there is a twist. I want you to think of things that can be made with paper that incorporate the characteristics of a fox. How can we make paper products incorporating these traits? How can it be marketed to customers? Take another two minutes to do this individually, and remember what I said earlier about self-criticism being the enemy of creativity: there are no bad ideas!"

Peter paused, pencil in hand as the rest of the group began writing. This was a challenge for him as he had never even attempted to link the characteristics of a fox with paper. He thought about what Pepe had said about no idea being a bad one, and got started.

OK, I can do this. What do I know about the fox? I think their fur is water resistant. How can that apply to-

Peter did not even need to finish his thought as he wrote his first idea down, "Water resistant paper." Peter even managed to think of a few other ideas, like bright red paper colored like a fox, and a paper jacket that is cold and water resistant, before Pepe called the group together.

"How did all of you do? What did you come up with?"

The DGD employees were excited to share their ideas with Pepe and called them out; "Red and white paper decorations!" "Furry paper hats!" "Paper cups that can keep a drink hot or cold!"

"Great ideas everyone! The ideas you created in this activity all fall within the third level of thinking, the creative level. Combining paper with the traits of a fox is surely new for all of you, but you pulled it off. This is called lateral thinking. It gets people to leave the familiar thinking levels of logic and memory, and enter the creative level. In order to think laterally, we often use objects or ideas to twist our thinking patterns - like we just used the fox. By thinking laterally we can come up with new, outside of the box ideas. Speaking of new ideas, it is time to switch from thinking about paper to thinking about Darn Good Donuts and new product, services and franchising ideas."

Peter glanced to the wall, where Pepe had taped a large piece of paper with the topic listed on it: *New Product or Service Ideas/New Franchising Opportunities*.

Pepe continued, "we are now going to combine all three levels of thinking. Please list ideas from memory, logical ideas, and try to find some radical or creative ideas, too. We are going to start with time for all of you to individually come up with ideas, so please take ten minutes or so to do this, and once again, no idea is a bad one!"

No idea is a bad one, reaffirmed Peter to himself. This time the ideas came quickly to him, and he was able to write down a dozen within the ten minute time period.

Stealing With Pride

At this point, Pepe instructed the DGD employees to form groups of three, and to then find and steal best ideas on their own piece of paper within those small groups. Peter found himself with two accountants from the finance department, Mikey and Michele.

"What do you got for us Peter? Anything good for me to take from you?", asked Mikey.

"Donut Kiosks," answered Peter confidently. "We currently franchise donut shops, so I was thinking we could offer something smaller and more accessible to first time franchisees. The kiosks could sell just a limited selection of our most popular products and can be placed just about anywhere."

"Good idea," encouraged Michele.

Peter was taken aback. Receiving encouragement for his creative ideas was not something he was used to, and he was beginning to enjoy himself as he, Michele, and Mikey continued to steal ideas from each other. They were soon interrupted by Pepe, who brought the whole group back together.

Story Time

"So far, so good everyone. I was paying attention to all of the groups and I saw that plenty of ideas were being stolen. Now before we form different small groups and continue stealing ideas, I want to take a quick break for a fun activity. Stay in the groups you currently are in. You are all going to tell a story together…but just one sentence at a time. The way it works is one person starts the story by saying just one thought or sentence. For example, 'once upon a time…'and then the next person continues with their own sentence. Keep the story going in your group for as long as you can. Any questions? No? Alright, go ahead!"

Peter didn't have enough time to complain or question the logic behind this seemingly silly game because Michele and Mikey jumped into the activity with enthusiasm. "Once upon a time there was a chef…" stated Mikey. "Who ate more than he cooked!", laughed Michele. They looked expectantly at Peter, who blurted out, "and because of this, he was very fat." "But he wanted a wife so he needed a diet," continued Mikey.

On and on Mikey, Michelle and Peter went, telling the story of a fat chef who wanted a wife and only ate asparagus and broccoli for months on end and then realized his true love and soulmate was…a jelly donut. They all had fun during this activity, and judging by the laughter in the room, so did the rest of the DGD crew.

"Great job everyone, I heard some amazing stories. Hopefully that activity woke your brains up a bit and to see if it did, take two minutes individually to try and write down more product development ideas for DGD."

Peter returned to his piece of paper, and found that he was able to think of two new ideas; a donut kitchen where people can come and pay to learn how to cook some of DGD's most popular donuts, and also a DGD apparel brand, where clothes featuring the company logo, and lots of cartoonish donuts could be marketed and sold. *A donut clothing line?* Peter thought to himself. *It seems kind of crazy, but it could work. You see all sorts of kids clothing with a cartoon caricature of just about anything on it, why not a Darn Good Donut?* Peter decided that the idea was good enough, as he remembered how Pepe stressed that self-criticism and doubt kill creativity.

Time to Steal Again

Pepe then had everyone form different small groups for the second round of idea sharing and stealing. Peter found two new colleagues to work with, Lorn and Joanna.

"The future of DGD is here," announced Lorn to Joanna and Peter. "Virtual donut shops! Just think of it, people can go online, and place an order to their 'neighborhood virtual donut shop', and in minutes, a baker's dozen of donuts delivered to their door."

"Interesting," commented Peter. "So the virtual donut shop is essentially a donut delivery service."

"Exactly right," agreed Lorn.

Peter shared his idea about DGD branded clothing, and he thought it was well received, despite being a bit off the wall. In fact, he noticed a trend in the ideas as Joanna was sharing her idea about donut related facial creams.

The ideas seem to be getting a bit more and more unusual. Virtual donut stores? Donut face and hand cream?! Strange…but it seems like maybe something of value is there nonetheless.

"Magnificent job everybody. I have conducted hundreds and hundreds of creativity sessions and I have yet to hear ideas like those I have been hearing so far today. I can tell you one thing though, it sure makes me want a donut," joked Pepe.

Who is the Best and Why: Benchmarking

"Once again we are going to temporarily change gears. Stay in the groups you currently are in. You have an assignment. Since part of our focus is on new franchising opportunities for DGD, I want you in your groups to think of a company which you believe does a great job at franchising. Once you have agreed on a company, spend some time trying to figure out why they are so successful. What do they do well? Please take five minutes to do this."

Lorn immediately proposed McDonalds as an example, and Peter and Joanna agreed. "Just think about it, McDonalds is everywhere, and instantly recognizable," pronounced Lorn.

"They seem to select their locations very carefully and in a calculated manner. I saw a McDonalds when I was driving on the way to the airport. It seemed like it was just placed on the side of the road, in a dead area, but when I passed it, sure enough there was a line of cars waiting for their food," added Peter.

And Joanna contributed, "don't forget their awesome French fries!"

The three continued to map out the components for success that they saw in McDonalds; consistent products, good locations, high market penetration, and so on.

Pepe then gave his next set of instructions. "What I want everyone to do now is to take the qualities for success that you found as a group, and think about how those qualities can relate to DGD. How can your products have the same components of success that you identified in other, very good franchising companies? This will be an individual task, so take about five minutes to think about this and then we will return to the topic of new product and franchising opportunities for DGD, and steal ideas one more time in different small groups."

Peter thought about what made McDonalds successful, and if that had anything that could be applied to DGD.

We both sell food, so I guess that is one similarity, at least on the surface level. One thing that makes them so unique is that they seem to represent familiarity...I know some people that take business trips halfway around the world, only to eat McDonalds...yes, I think the customer always knows what to expect, it is a known quantity. We could look at placing stores in new locations, like airports and transit centers, and then launch a marketing campaign to try and tap into this idea of familiarity in unfamiliar territories, something that has worked so well for McDonalds.

Never before had Peter thought about ad campaigns, and deeper meanings, like familiarity in food, but he was now. Pepe soon announced that it was time to form small groups for the third time and have one last round of stealing.

Even More Stealing

This time, Peter found himself working with Tameka and Aldo. Peter shared his idea about stores in airports. Tameka had an idea that Peter did not even imagine possible.

"Healthy donuts."

Aldo thought he had misheard and that she had said something like heavy donuts, and his jaw dropped when he realized what she was on to.

"Yes you heard me right. I know that after work I always eat a protein bar before I go to the gym…why can't I be eating a protein donut instead?"

"Protein donuts, I am definitely stealing that," Aldo said eagerly. "You may have just found our golden ticket, or a path to bankruptcy and the unemployment line. How did you think of the idea?"

Tameka replied, "In the last activity when we were thinking about companies good at franchising and what makes them successful, I was thinking about World Fitness, a chain of gyms. They are popular because everyone wants to be healthy and as fit as possible these days, it is the popular thing to do. So, I thought protein donuts could be our ticket."

"That really is a great idea," said Peter, as Aldo nodded in agreement.

Pepe once again grabbed the group's attention. "It is just about time to choose the best ideas and show them to the entire group, but I have one final activity for you all to do first. You can stay in the groups you currently are in to do this.

SCAMPER

This activity is called SCAMPER. The word itself is not important in figuring out what this activity is, the important thing is what each letter represents. S is for substitute, C is for combine. A stands for adapt and M stands for modify. P means put to other use. E is for eliminate and R is for rearrange. I know that is a lot to keep track of, but don't worry, each group is only going to focus on one letter. What I want you to do is focus on the idea represented by the letter, and how it can be applied to the DGD products and stores that exist today. If your group gets the letter E, you will think of what can be eliminated from the DGD product line, or stores. If your group gets the letter R for rearrange, you can think about if things can be done in a different order. This can be from a business perspective, or from how a customer uses your product. And I know I don't need to remind any of you to be creative and to embrace any and all ideas."

Pepe quickly assigned letters to each of the small groups, and he gave Peter, Tameka, and Aldo's group the letter S, which stands for substitute."

By this stage of the session, Peter was feeling downright enthusiastic about this whole creativity movement and he decided to take charge, leading his group in discussion. "What can we substitute?"

"I think that is what we just discussed with my idea for healthy donuts. We are substituting unhealthy food for health food," said Tameka.

"How about if we substitute plastic chairs, and a quick, informal atmosphere for fine dining?" Aldo asked. "Think about it. Donut fine dining. I was watching TV the other day and I saw a show about a restaurant where people pay $50 a plate to eat something called gourmet fast-food. It is basically just burgers, fries and pizza, but fancier versions. We could do the same with donuts."

Peter laughed, thinking about Michelin Stars and donuts together, and said, "Why not?"

After a few more moments of discussion, the SCAMPER activity ended, and Pepe told everyone work in their small groups and to agree on the best ideas that they heard during the session.

Peter and his group members were all very excited about the idea of healthy donuts, and agreed that the best idea that they would put forth as a group would be Superfood and Protein donuts.

S	Substitute	Look at things in a new way by trying to substitute a part of the existing product with something else.
C	Combine	Streamline your product or process by trying to combine features or parts.
A	Adapt	What things can be adapted or changed to better fit the existing climate or to address a problem?
M	Modify/ Distort	Modify or distort the existing product or process into something new. What changes can be made to take a product and change it to fit into a different market or context?
P	Put to other use	What other uses are there for the existing product? What other markets can it be sold in because of this new use?
E	Eliminate	Simplify things by removing a part of the process or product. By eliminating aspects and simplifying things, new opportunities and ideas emerge.
R	Rearrange	What would things be like if the problem/ product/process worked in reverse or was done in a different order? What would you do if you had to do it in reverse? You can use this to see your problem from different angles and come up with new ideas.

Figure 28: The SCAMPER activity is great for developing an already existing product, service, process or idea.

"Just imagine," said Tameka, as Peter was writing the idea down on a large piece of paper to be displayed at the front of the room. "Gyms and health food stores could franchise a mini DGD stand featuring the healthy donuts."

"Tasty and healthy, the best of both worlds," agreed Aldo.

Peter went to the front of the room and taped the piece of paper to the wall where seven other ideas were already posted. Pepe, seeing that all the groups had finished the activity and posted their ideas on the wall, brought the session to a close.

"Let's see what we think are the best new product, service and franchising opportunities for DGD, shall we? I see healthy donuts, a donut social club, donut kitchens and cooking schools, DGD branded clothing, DGD health clubs, DGD food carts, and finally DGD daycare."

Wow, my idea for DGD apparel was selected, that's pretty neat, thought Peter to himself. *I guess it makes sense though, with all the changing of groups we did there ought to be a consensus of sorts. It is like they tell the donut chefs in the DGD cooking school, a good donut always rises above the rest. I guess it is the same with ideas.*

There was a round of comments evaluating the results of the creativity workshop and a short discussion. Everyone seemed excited about the ideas. Pepe instructed, "to finish today's session, there is one thing left to do. On you way out of the room when you are leaving, take a look at all of the ideas posted on the wall and sign your name under the idea or ideas that you want to work on. Now that we have the future of DGD here, you just need to decide on which of these magnificent ideas you want to focus on. But the details in that are best left for another day. Today, just supporting an idea by signing your name is enough. Thanks again to each and every one of you for a great creativity session."

Peter began neatly organizing his things and packing up. He watched as the other DGD employees crowed around the ideas at the front of the room and was startled by his own thoughts; *I can't wait for the next creativity session.*

Analysis: What Happened Here?

Creativity sessions help people create new ideas that can sometimes turn out to be huge successes. Creativity sessions also do something else that is just as important; they give people the opportunity to share ideas that have existed all along, which often are ideas that come from the *memory level* of thinking. These memory level ideas may have been implemented or used before, only to be abandoned for one reason or another. It is important to realize that while new, extraordinary ideas are a good result of creativity sessions, giving ideas that already exist within the group a chance to be heard is just as important.

To bring forth ideas and promote creativity in the most effective way possible, I relied on a combination of two different tools, both with their own strengths and that when used together, are very powerful.

Lateral Thinking and Idealogue: Two Ingredients for Creativity

The structure of this session is very different than what we have seen in previous chapters. In Chapter 5, the problem solving chapter where we visited Soundless Components in Beijing, we combined tools and used Root Cause Analysis along with Idealogue. But we only used root cause analysis in the beginning of the session during the initial individual stage. After that point, the session followed the Idealogue structure; repeated group formation and idea sharing and stealing.

On the other hand, the creativity session we just visited followed a very different format; different tools and activities were given between each round of group formation and idea stealing.

The activities given throughout the creativity session all come from the same family of tools, called lateral thinking Tools. Remember Edward de Bono and his three levels of thinking? He also is the creator of the term lateral thinking. According to De Bono, lateral thinking is key because it allows us to escape the first two levels of thinking; the memory level and the logical level. Ideas that come from these levels are perfectly valid and important, but they also can hurt the creative process because most of our ideas are based on memory and logic. If we are asked to think of new ideas or something abstract or outside of the box, we often try to rely on our memory or logical thinking to do so, and we end up with the same old ideas as always, and not something new. De Bono sums up the importance of lateral thinking with the following analogy, saying that you cannot dig a new whole by digging the same hole deeper[7].

---

[7] This quote is taken directly from Edward de Bono's webpage, which I highly recommend visiting: http://www.edwdebono.com/#!lateral-thinking/ge9l2

- Edward de Bono was born in 1933 in Malta.
- He invented the term 'lateral thinking', and first wrote about it in the book "The Use of Lateral Thinking", published in 1967.
- He has published over 50 books, which have been translated into dozens of languages.
- De Bono was nominated for the Nobel Prize for Economics in 1995.
- He does not focus on working with one specific group. Instead, he works with everyone from young children to distinguished academics and world leaders.

Figure 29: Edward de Bono is a pioneer in conceptualizing how thinking and creativity work.

By mixing in lateral thinking tools in between rounds of idea stealing, several important things are achieved. First off, the tools serve as icebreakers and work wonders at relaxing the participants. Tension and nervousness are two natural enemies of creativity. Have you ever been in bed, at the point of falling asleep and then think of a new idea or have inspiration strike you? I know I have, and I have heard many others confirm the same thing. One chief reason for this is that you are calm and relaxed, and therefore more open to new thoughts and ideas. Creativity comes in a relaxed state. By using lateral thinking tools repeatedly throughout the session, the third level of thinking is promoted and people are more relaxed, which is crucial. Relaxed people are also much more capable of working in groups and sharing ideas too, so the lateral thinking activities also directly improve the quality of the group sharing sessions.

What Tools Were Used?

By now I hope that I have convinced you that lateral thinking tools are very important and very powerful, especially when paired with Idealogue. But how do these tools work and how to decide when to use them within a creativity session? In this section I will review each of the tools used during the session, explaining their specific purpose and how you can use them most effectively.

First Things First: Introducing Different Levels of Thinking

The very first lateral thinking tool that I used served as a way to introduce de Bono's three levels of thinking. I began the session by having everyone write down all the possible uses that they could think of for a sheet of paper. Once they had completed the task, I asked for some examples of what they came up with, and I then showed how the first examples most people think of come from memory or logic. Then de Bono and his three levels of thinking were introduced. The aim of doing this is for everyone to relate directly to the three levels of thinking and experience the tendency stay within the memory and logic levels. Explaining de Bono's levels of thinking also helps people better understand different types of ideas and how they are produced, be it from experience (memory), logic, or lateral thinking (creative).

Getting the group to understand these different levels makes it possible for me to tell a group that ideas based on the memory level are equally important as creative ones," which is something I want the group to understand. Ideas from the memory level are often ignored. When participants come to a creativity session they may have been thinking about ways of developing their work and they have been experimenting with many ideas that did not fly for dozens of years. When participants are asked to think of new ideas, this whole category of ideas is ignored. In the many creativity sessions I have overseen, the easiest ideas to implement are ones that have existed all along. People were just lacking the place and time to share, discuss and develop them.

This activity also serves as a good introductory icebreaker and warms people up for the upcoming activities. It also allows me to provide everyone with a definition of creativity, and to make sure the group is starting with a similar approach to creativity. If I were to just launch directly into the session, saying things like "be creative!", it may not work because *creativity* is an ambiguous term. I also did this in the visioning session that we visited in chapter 4; I defined specifically what I meant by 'common vision' to ensure that the group shared some common ground as the session got underway.

Paper and Foxes: A Forced Connection

Immediately after defining the creative level of thinking I gave the group an activity that would force them to think creatively. I asked someone to name an animal that they liked, (in this example a fox), and I then had the group individually list ideas on how to market paper products using the qualities of a fox. The specific prompts of 'paper' and 'foxes' are unimportant. Any topics can be used. This activity also shows the difference between ideas based on the memory and logic levels versus ideas belonging to the creativity level. Oftentimes ideas based on logic or memory are not talked about or searched for in creativity sessions, as they already exist and are inherently obvious within the day to day business climate.

Presumably no one has explored such ideas on their own, and asking the group to think about this topic forced people to connect two unrelated topics in their mind. This connection is a forced connection, and the ideas people think of in this phase all fall under the third level of thinking; the creative level. This immediately shows the group what it feels like to think on this level, and completing the activity gives confidence that they can do it.

At this point I guide the focus back to the topic that the creativity session is built around. In the example with DGD, it was to think of new products, services and franchising ideas. Around ten minutes is given for people to list ideas individually, and after this is completed, they are put into small groups of three to share and steal these ideas.

Story Time

Once the group had a chance to share and steal ideas about the day's topic, I gave them a group activity called the rotating story. Here people were instructed to work in their small groups and tell a story with each person supplying one line of the story at a time. The rotating story activity can even be done with people giving one word at a time instead of an entire line, if you want to really challenge people. That is just a small detail. What is important about this activity is that it forces people to be quick on their feet and provides a nice warm up for the group activities that come later on. There is usually a lot of laughter during the rotating story, as people just cannot resist trying to be funny and tell entertaining stories. I have said it before and I will say it again here; creativity flows much easier when people are relaxed. That is the main point of including this activity in the creativity session; it relaxes people for the important topics yet to come. Immediately after the rotating story, I tell people to try and think of even more ideas about what new product and franchising opportunities there are for DGD. You would be surprised by how many new ideas people can come up with after taking a break and playing a thinking game like the rotating story.

Benchmarking, Client Experience and Trend Analysis: Making Creativity Real

Before continuing with the next round of sharing and stealing in new small groups, I gave an activity called Benchmarking. The instructions for this activity were for people to think of a company that they feel do a great job at franchising, and then think of why that is. In other words, what company can be thought of as the benchmark for franchising success and why? Since the topic of the day included new ideas about franchising opportunities for DGD, I chose a prompt related to franchising. If I were holding a session with the topic being, 'best viral marketing company', I would ask for people to think of a great example of a viral marketing campaign or company, and why they thought that it was successful. The prompt of the benchmarking activity typically relates somehow to the topic of the creativity session.

De Bono's levels of thinking: Define and explain the levels- memory, logic, and creativity -to the group. The purpose is to make sure you will get ideas from all levels and thus a larger number of ideas to start with.

Rotating Story: Telling a story together, one sentence at a time. You may start with: Once upon a time...
This activity relaxes the group and helps them create new ideas.

Benchmarking: Define what the best companies do well.
To create new ideas based on real world success.

SCAMPER: Give the group questions based on the letters.
You may use this tool to redesign an already existing product, process, or idea, by changing one aspect of it.

Idealogue: Steal with Pride! The purpose of this tool is to help participants connect their ideas.

Figure 30: The tools used in the creativity session.

After the employees of DGD were given time to think of an example of a good franchising company and that company's traits for success, I then related it back to their own product and asked them to come up with even more ideas for their own company using the company and traits that they came up with during the benchmarking activity. This activity not only produces creative ideas, but goes a step further by forcing people to think of ideas based on real world success. This leads to more concrete ideas that are more likely to succeed.

I chose to use the benchmarking activity during my session with DGD, but there are two other lateral thinking tools that can help generate creative ideas linked to the real world.

The first is called trends analysis. Instead of asking for the group to think of a company that they deem the benchmark of their industry, I ask for people to think of large trends that are occurring within their industry or business market. The trends can be consumer or business trends and behavior. Once everyone has a few trends in mind, I ask them to revisit the day's topic and to try and think of more ideas based on these trends. We saw a bit of this type of thinking in the DGD example with Tameka, who thought of the healthy donut idea. She mentioned how it was popular for people to be health conscious these days, which gave her the idea of producing and selling healthy donuts.

Another variant of this activity is called the 'client experience.' As you may have guessed, the prompt this time is the customer. I ask people to think of the entire process of how a person interacts with their company. If I used this activity with DGD, someone would have thought of a person first getting a craving for a donut, then driving to the nearest DGD store, walking in, smelling the donuts, making up their mind that they wanted two maple bars, buying them and then eating them, along with a DGD coffee. The prompt for this activity can be just about anything; you the facilitator can be creative too! You can ask for people to tell a story, draw a picture, or map out their own experience as a customer using a product, and then relate that back to the topic at hand.

Trends analysis: Think of current trends in your market or pop culture. What are they?

This activity helps you capitalize on current trends .

Client experience: Write down or draw how a client interacts with your product/company. What are the stages for them? What is the client feeling during different stages?

This activity helps create more client oriented products or services.

Figure 31: Additional tools that can be used in creativity sessions.

Once people had their version of the client experience in mind, they would have an idea of how the client behaves and interacts with their product. With this information in mind I would ask people to revisit the topic of the day and try to think of even more ideas, in the case of the DGD example, new product, service or franchising opportunities.

As mentioned, the client experience activity, the benchmarking activity and the trends analysis activity are important tools because they result in creative ideas based around real factors.

SCAMPER: A Lateral Thinking Tool Loved by Logical Thinkers

SCAMPER focuses on modifying an existing product, business, or idea, instead of radically reinventing the wheel. With clear, concise instructions, the activity assigns one of seven questions to challenge small groups to review, redesign and reimagine something that already exists. With SCAMPER, people are focusing on only changing one aspect of something tangible, something that is already real, and this makes the activity feels less abstract for participants. One interesting trend that I have seen time and time again in creativity sessions is the positive reaction to the SCAMPER activity by engineers. The specific instructions of this activity seem to appeal to them, and to other analytical thinkers. By balancing out the complete freedom of the forced connections activity with a more technical lateral thinking tool you can be sure to appeal to a range of thinking styles.

> The SCAMPER method was born out of the genius of two men; Alex Osborn and Bob Eberle. Osborn was very influential in developing early forms of brainstorming, and he formed many of the questions and unique angles of viewing things that are now used in the SCAMPER method. Eberle took these questions and organized them into the format that is now known as SCAMPER.

Figure 32: The roots of SCAMPER.

Ending the Session

You may have noticed that the session ended rather quickly. Once the best ideas were selected, there was no debate about how to actualize these ideas, and I did not ask the group to rank or prioritize the ideas. I just had people sign their names under an idea that they were interested in, and I left it at that. This is by design. Developing the ideas further requires a different focus, and is best left for another session which may follow immediately or take place later on. Today with the creativity session, the point is to just produce the ideas without criticism or analysis.

Why Idealogue?

After all this talk about how wonderful the lateral thinking tools are, you may be asking, "Well why not just have a creativity session based solely on these tools? Why do we even need Idealogue here?"

While trying to not sound too philosophical, I will answer that question with a question of my own; what is an unshared idea worth? Not much. While the results and out of the box ideas produced by the lateral thinking activities are valuable and useful, sometimes the real treasure of a creativity session is just getting people to talk in a creative context and giving them the opportunity to share their ideas.

The great thing about combining lateral thinking tools with Idealogue is that the strengths of Idealogue cancel out the weaknesses of lateral thinking tools and vice versa. Idealogue is great at getting people to exchange ideas and understand each other's ideas, but it does not promote creativity without the help of other tools. Lateral thinking tools allow for people to think of some pretty crazy ideas, but without the help of Idealogue it is hard for people to understand and share these crazy ideas with each other. But combining these two types of tools can lead to amazing results, as I have seen time and time again.

Chapter 8
Actioning

A normal Friday afternoon involves me sitting in Helsinki traffic, most likely watching rain or snow fall onto my windscreen. But today was much different. I was not worried about traffic or snow. Instead my mind kept returning to one singular thought; akara. What is akara and why was I obsessing over it? Akara is a delicious fried bean cake, which is one of Nigeria's most well-known culinary delights. And the reason I was thinking about it? Because I was not in Helsinki, I was in Lagos, working with the Assorted Nigeria Limited team.

You may remember Esther, Sam Adebayo, Wilfred and the rest of the Assorted Nigerian Limited employees from the visioning session I had with them, which was covered in Chapter 4 of this book. During the visioning session, the Assorted Nigeria Limited employees agreed that a unified company was key, and through unification they could expand into other markets outside of Nigeria and also improve the performance of some of their products, resulting in Assorted Nigeria Limited's products leading their respective markets. They even managed to produce a great vision statement for the future during the visioning session; "Assorted Nigeria Limited is the crowned eagle of the African market: Soaring above the competition as a unified family."

The next day I led the Assorted Nigeria Limited team in a strategy session where the team was able to think of company strategies that could help Assorted

Nigeria Limited reach its goal of becoming more united and a market leader. The strategies they came up with were to move all production to Lagos, and to narrow their product catalog down to the items that are performing at the top of their markets, or that have the potential to do so.

Instead of six factories spread all over the country, the Assorted Nigeria Limited employees thought it would be a better strategy to have three factories in Lagos focusing on the best performing items; children's toys, pet food, and pens.

Beginning the Session

As I prepared to begin the session, I looked once more at the group joining me. Just like last time, there was the president and CEO Sam Adebayo impeccably dressed in a stylish suit. Next to Sam sat Esther, the COO, and who was in a lot of ways the woman behind the scenes who ensured that the business ran smoothly. Next to her sat the quiet accountant Ade. The rest of the group was rounded out by the people who were going to be most affected by the new strategy: the factory managers. And sure enough, Eve, Alex, Wilfred, Moses, John and Cecilia all seemed slightly on edge as we were about to begin.

"Good morning everyone! I hope you all feel as rested and excited as I do today. Before we get started, can some of you quickly recap the strategies that you came up with during yesterday's strategic session?"

Sam Adebayo spoke first and began to explain the changes. Then several of the factory workers spoke in turn, informing me of the products that will be discontinued, and specifying that pens, children's toys, and pet food were going be the focus from here on out. As these points were covered, I summarized by writing key words on the large paper flipchart at the front of the room. After a few more minutes of listening and writing while the strategic decisions were discussed, a nice summary of the strategic actions was created.

- Only continue production of pens, children's toys and pet food
- Close down and sell all factories located outside of Lagos
- Centralize production/employees to Lagos
- Explore potential to market and sell products in foreign markets
- Have weekly team meetings
- Expand HR department

Figure 33: The paper flip chart at the front of the room summarizing the strategy of Assorted Nigeria Limited.

"Do you all agree on the summarized key strategic points?" I asked.

The Assorted Nigeria team nodded yes, so I continued.

"The first thing I want all of you to do is think about what you personally will do to help make the strategy a reality. What are the logical steps for you regarding this strategic process? Do not worry if you are thinking of the 'correct' actions or not. All things that you need to do, professional or personal, big or small, are important to make note of. Take about ten minutes to do this individually and then we will reconvene as a group."

As soon as the instructions were out of my mouth, the group got started. I could see that some people were writing extremely quickly, while others seemed to take their time. This made sense not just because people work at different speeds, but also because the strategic changes had a relatively minor effect on some, while greatly affecting others.

I glanced at one of the people writing at a casual pace; John Ambrose. John was currently running the pet food factory in Lagos. His product was still going to be produced, and in the same factory. The same was true for Wilfred, who ran the children's toys factory in Lagos.

On the other end of the spectrum were those who had to relocate to Lagos and move their factories, or even worse, cease production of their products and either leave the company or transition into a new role within Assorted Nigerian Limited. One of these people was Alex Musa, who was writing at a frenzied pace. He was in charge of the pen factory in Ibadan. He soon would be following the production of pens to Lagos, where they were going to be made in the factory that used to be the Lagos cosmetics factory, formally ran by Eve Ebi. *I am sure that Alex and Eve have a lot on their minds* I thought, while looking at my watch. Sure enough, ten minutes had already passed. The beginning individual stage had just ended.

"Now take a moment and find two other people to chat with. Just like last time, we will have three rounds of 'stealing with pride', in different groups of three each time. This time you will have twenty minutes for stealing in each group. In your groups, explain what actions you will take in order to implement the new Assorted Nigeria Limited strategies, learn from others and develop the action points together."

With this said, groups of three were formed. Moses, Ade, and Eve were in a group directly in front of me, so I was able to hear a bit of what they had to say.

"For me these changes are paper based," said Ade, the head accountant. "It has been so long since Assorted Nigeria Limited has sold assets on a large scale, so there is much for me to do in learning what forms are needed, what legalities need to be addressed, and what I can do so we make these transactions as easy as possible."

"So for you it is basically business as usual," interjected Moses.

Ade replied, "Yes and no. A lot of the changes will bring me into unfamiliar territory. But it is true that this unfamiliar territory is still within the financial and accounting realm. I will be filing reports to the same agencies and commissions. The main change for me is the content of what I will be filing. So one of my first actions is to learn about this by doing some research. Also, since we will be cutting production activity all regions outside of Lagos, there will need to be some closure of regional accounts. I am not too aware of how this works, but I have some accountant friends of mine who are well versed in the topic, and I will be able to discuss this with them over dinner."

"Wow Ade, accounting talk over dinner, that sounds like my dream Friday night," joked Moses.

"To each their own. What about you two?" asked Ade.

"Well, I think my actions may require a bit more social skills than yours do Ade. I first have to convince my wife and children to leave the comfort of Kano and relocate to Lagos. My wife is from Kano, you know. I have convinced them that this move is necessary, but that does not mean it will be an easy process for them. So that is my first action ahead of all the stuff related to the business; make my family feel comfortable with this change. If I don't manage to do this, then there is no point in planning out what I need to do on the professional side."

Ade and Eve gave Moses sympathetic looks, and Eve had an idea. "You and your family will not be the only people going through this change, Moses. Think of all the other families within Assorted Nigeria Limited who also will be relocating here. Maybe some type of family meet up or outside of work activity can be arranged so that new people in Lagos will not feel so alone or isolated."

Ade added, "I have lived here my whole life, and I know a lot about the city, so if there are any questions about how things work here, I can help. Also, I think that my son is about the same age as your children, so naturally you can tell them that while they will be leaving friends behind in Kano, they will be able to look forward to meeting new friends here in Lagos."

Moses looked like he felt more comfortable with the prospect of relocating his family, and thanked Ade and Eve, adding, "with these ideas, I think my wife and children will be happier about this change. What about you Eve? What actions are you going to take?"

"Well at least I get to stay in Lagos, so where I live will not change. But I feel like everything else does though. My factory will be converted into a pen factory, and I assume the old factory manager Alex will be taking over operations. So I will be looking to have a new role within the company. But before I can do this, as factory manager I need to look out for the workers in my factory. My first action is to meet with them to see if they wish to continue. I also need to talk to Sam and see what positions are available. We are closing down a lot of factories, so I assume that a lot of factory workers will be out of a job."

"Don't be so sure Eve," Ade chimed in. "Although we are focusing on just three products now, we want those three products to be market leaders, so I think that we will need to increase the production quantity of these three products to make that happen. While I am sure that not everyone working in factories outside of Lagos will want to try and relocate here to stay with the company, there still may be lots of opportunity for those who wish to stay."

Moses and Eve agreed, and Eve continued to explain her actions.

"After I meet with all my factory workers and see what opportunities there are for them, I need to focus on what I want to do within the company. If I am not working in producing cosmetics, I do not want to continue running a factory. Plus, I think that Alex will do a great job and he can take charge with the pen production here."

"Where does that leave you?" asked Ade.

"Well, one of our strategies is to further develop HR. I want to work on that, so my first action is to talk with Sam, and then email the rest of the company to see if anyone else is interested in helping out with developing HR."

Moses said, "I can see you doing that easily. You are very conscious of others, I mean your first action is to worry about your factory workers before sorting yourself out. You have the heart needed for the job."

Eve was grateful for Moses's compliments, and thanked him for the kind words. I was very happy, listening to Ade, Eve and Moses's conversation. They were sharing their actions with each other, offering encouragement, and also presenting themselves as allies and sources of support for one another. In other words, things were going exactly as they should be. At this point I snapped back to reality and realized that I needed to stop eavesdropping, and continue leading the session.

"Nice work everybody, I would not expect anything less from this group. It is time for round two of group sharing, so find two new people to work with and spend another twenty minutes sharing your individual actions with them."

Another round of sharing in small groups went on, and after another thirty minutes, I instructed the group to form small groups once again for the final round.

Just like I witnessed during the first round of sharing by watching Moses, Ade, and Eve, I saw collaboration, and the further development of action points in the subsequent small group sharing sessions. John and Sam Adebayo both offered tips and support to Cecilia. Cecilia, the manager of the rubber tire valve factory in Abuja which was closing down, knew a lot about foreign markets which Assorted Nigeria Limited hoped to enter in the future. Cecilia wanted to develop action points related to the outlined strategy of 'explore the potential to sell Assorted Nigeria Limited products in foreign markets', but she was a bit shaky on what actions she could specifically take. John offered up some of his contacts he had in Ghana and Cameroon, and the big boss Sam immediately scheduled a meeting with Cecilia so that the two of them could spend some time to make a plan for how she could best act on the foreign market strategy. Cecilia, to put it mildly, was thrilled.

During the final two rounds of sharing, ideas became more streamlined and refined as they were shared, and re-shared. By the end of the third round, I saw that everyone seemed to have in mind what practical, useful actions they were going to take in the following days and weeks to help actualize the new strategies.

On the Road to Success

"It looks like all of you are ready to leave right now and begin immediately on the new actions you have created for yourselves. You will be able to do that very soon, but not quite yet. There is one final thing I would like all of you to do. As I pass out these large post-it notes, I want you to think of what you personally will do next regarding the strategy. What are the best, most important actions for you to take regarding the bigger picture? If you have more than one action in mind, then write one action on a large post-it and then take another post-it for the next action. More than one action is OK. You should talk about this in the small groups you are in, and when you are ready, write your actions on post-it notes and place them on this beautiful roadmap I have drawn on the flipchart at the front of the room. Each action posted needs to be detailed and have a clear 'who', 'what', and 'when.' "

I pulled back the flipchart to reveal my simple drawing of a roadmap. On the chart I had drawn a road, running upwards from the lower left corner to the upper right. On the bottom left corner, I wrote the word *now*, in the middle I wrote *1 to 3 months*, and on the bottom right corner I wrote *4 months or longer*.

"When you place the post-it note with your action written on it on this page, I want you to think about when it will occur. If it is something you will begin with immediately, then please place it on the left side, closer to the word *now*. If it is something for you to do later on, then it belongs on the right side, closer to *4 months or longer*. Once all of the post-it notes have been placed on the roadmap, we will have a complete picture of what all of your actions look like together."

"I still don't get it, are we writing individual or group actions?" asked Abe.

"You may write individual or group actions in your groups, meaning that your post-it may have just one name or multiple names. However, you may not write actions for people who are not in your group of three unless you ask their permission," I replied.

"I have an action for the real estate agent to find me a new home in Lagos, what do I do with that one?" asked Moses.

"You could write an action point for yourself Moses. Something like: 'I will contact a real estate agent to sell my house. Name: Moses Time: tomorrow.' "

Everyone took a few moments for discussion in their groups, and one by one actions were written down, and then posted on the roadmap. After a while, the task was finished and we all stood around the roadmap, admiring the completed picture. The group of nine had managed to post a total of 33 different post-it notes on the roadmap. Some people only contributed one action while others had three or four different actions to stick on the board. The specific number of actions posted by a person was not important though, instead what mattered is that everyone had something to contribute to the roadmap.

Getting Feedback...with a Whip

After the roadmap activity was completed, I was not finished with the group yet.

"You all seem pleased with the roadmap," I told the group.

"No disrespect, but you don't have to be a genius to see that Pepe," said Moses, as the rest of the group chuckled.

"Good point Moses, but I still need to make sure. Now that all of you are here standing, we are going to have a round of feedback. Do you all remember the activity last time where I asked you to hold up one to 5 fingers to give feedback based on how you felt about the visioning content?"

The group did indeed remember, so I continued.

"Well this time I would like to get feedback from you all about how well the content on the roadmap relates to the new Assorted Nigeria Limited strategies. Are these actions going to help achieve the strategies? Do they make sense to you?"

Sam Adebayo, Ade, and Cecilia jumped the gun a bit, and were already holding five fingers in the air. I was pleased by their eagerness, but I had a twist on how I wanted the feedback.

"This time, instead of getting holding up fingers to show your feedback, we are going to go around in a circle, and each person will say one word to voice their feedback. The words you can choose from are; terrible, bad, average, good, or great. No explanation of your choice is needed, all I want from each of you is just one word. This activity is called the whip, because your feedback is going to cut around the room quickly, like a whip. Ready?"

The group was full of quick learners, and the feedback whip raced around the room.

"Great" "Great" "Good" "Great" "Great" "Good" "Average" "Good" "Great"

"Fantastic everyone. Can someone who rated the content of today as "great" explain why?"

- Have everyone stand in a circle or semi-circle.
- Give a feedback prompt or a set of words/numbers they can choose from.
- One person starts and gives their one word answer, and feedback continue around the room.
- Ask people for elaboration on why they scored as they did.
- This feedback tool is named called, "WHIP" because feedback is intended to travel around the room like a whip: quick and sharp (honest feedback).

Figure 34: The feedback Whip is a fun way to get rapid group feedback.

Sam Adebayo replied, "I scored the content as great because I now see how everything fits. The strategies we produced on our own during the strategy session were important, but they did not seem possible. Or maybe they seemed possible, but there were a significant amount of questions about how we would achieve them. For me those questions have now been answered."

I thanked Sam for his words, and asked those who scored the content good to elaborate, and I then asked the same question relating to the "average" score. I was not worried about the scores people gave, and I was not looking for unanimous agreement either. I just wanted to give everyone a chance to speak their mind. If someone did have a problem with the roadmap and noticed an error in the timeline, or if two actions posted separately could be combined, then the changes could be made together as a group during or after the feedback round.

The sun was perched high in the sky, which meant that the time was already well into the afternoon and that it was time to bring this session to a close.

"I had a great time working with all of you, and I want to thank Assorted Nigeria Limited for asking me to Lagos. I think that our work is done here, and I want you to keep this roadmap that you made today somewhere on your premises where it is visible. The actions on this roadmap are the direct path to reaching your new strategic goals, and I wish all of you luck on that journey."

Cecilia, Eve, Moses, and the rest of the gang thanked me, and ended my day in the best way possible, by suggesting that we all go out together and have an early dinner of akara.

Analysis: What happened here?

The whole point of an actioning session is to produce concrete actions on an individual level that can combine with the actions of others to form a group level plan of action. This plan of action is then used to turn strategic goals into reality. In the session we just witnessed, I used a common actioning activity, the roadmap, along with Idealogue. As we have seen before and as we will see again, using Idealogue with other tools maximizes the chances of success, and produces content in the most effective way. Before I go into further detail about the tools used in this session, I need to congratulate Assorted Nigeria Limited for a forward thinking approach to their actioning session. No, I am not congratulating them for being smart enough to invite me to help, I cannot take that credit even if I would like to. I am referring to them adopting a participatory approach to decision making. There is a direct correlation between group participation and commitment. Take the actions that the group produced and placed on the roadmap during the session. They were thought of as a group, and people were excited about them.

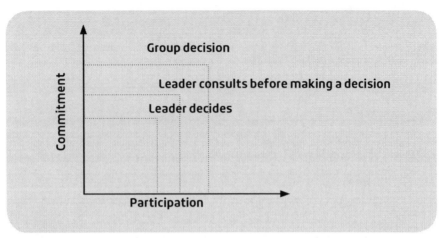

Figure 35: The more people are involved in the decision-making process, the more committed they are.

Most importantly, all of the actions together formed a sensible plan. If these exact same logical actions were not produced as a group and instead handed down from the top, directly from the desk of Sam Adebayo, they would not have the same effect and most likely they would not succeed. If the facilitator would have taken one strategy at a time and asked for someone to take responsibility, which is actually a common practice by the way, there would be very few volunteers and there would not be much participation and therefore less taking responsibility and less commitment. It is more effective for employees to be at least consulted before decisions are made, and it is even better if decisions and actions are decided on and produced in a group setting, using Idealogue. In order to make it easier to volunteer and to take responsibility, I always start actioning with individual actions which together will form the group actions. If you want to make sure that each strategy or solution will have understandable and concrete actions, you can review the points together as a group at the end of the session and add additional action points if necessary.

What Tools Were Used: Beginning the Session Right: a Warm-up and Review

In the beginning of the session I first had the group briefly explain to me what their new strategies were. I did this for two reasons.

First, I wanted to get people talking and warmed up. Never underestimate how important a warm-up activity is; it relaxes people, gets them talking, and gets them comfortable.

The second reason is to create a common definition of what the company strategies were. I could assume that everyone was on the same page concerning their new strategies, but it never hurts to make sure, and for a group to come up with individual actions that are compatible with the other actions, I needed to make sure everyone had the same strategic points in mind.

The Roadmap: You Can Be Lost Without It

It is great for people to think of actions on an individual level, and the individual level is needed. Not all actions can be produced in a group. We saw the example of Moses being extremely concerned for how the company changes would affect his family, and making them comfortable and integrating them into life in Lagos was the most important action point for him. If this does not happen, then nothing else does for Moses. If all actions were produced as a group, then Moses' concerns would not be addressed and he would be left feeling that the actions decided for him would not correctly represent what he needs to do.

On the other hand, ending an actioning session without combining everyone's individual action points would be a mistake too. This is why the road mapping activity is an important part of the session.

Figure 36: The roadmap lets everyone see the larger picture, uniting the individual actions to a greater whole.

The road mapping activity makes the individual actions of everyone more concrete, and more likely to happen. If you have a personal goal, you can keep it to yourself and work very hard to achieve it. Maybe you will. But if you write your goal down, then you have a better chance of making it come true. And if you really want to make your goal come true, then write it down, share it with others, and display it in a public place. This is what the roadmap activity effectively does.

It also contextualizes the personal action points by placing them onto a timeline. Do they happen now or will they happen later on in the future? The roadmap allows for people to decide.

Finally, the roadmap combines individual action points with those of others, creating a complete picture of what will be done. People can easily see what others will be doing, what separate action points can be combined and collaborated on, and which action points are dependent on others.

End the Session with Feedback: Using the WHIP

In Chapter 4 I explained the importance of getting feedback from a group. This lets me know how the session went for the group, and it also gives people one final chance to voice any concerns or give any comments about the content, and the session in general. This time I used a tool called "the whip" to ask for feedback.

To use this tool, you first need everyone together as one large group. You explain how a whip moves-fast and sharp, and that you want their feedback to be the same. Fast in the sense that each person will only say one word, and as soon as one person has spoken, the next person continues immediately so that the feedback goes around the room quickly, and uncensored. The fact that the feedback is uncensored and honest is what makes it sharp. A variety of things can be used as the options for what words the group can choose from. With Assorted Nigeria Limited, I asked them to choose a word from either "terrible, bad, average, good, or great." You can choose different words, a numeric scale from one to five, or you may even let the participants choose one word that best describes their feeling towards the results.

Why Idealogue in Actioning Sessions?

An effective actioning session needs more than just people thinking of their action points individually and then placing them on a roadmap, it needs Idealogue. By having people repeatedly share their action points in small groups, people gain confidence, new allies and sources of support are discovered, and the actions are made real.

By repeatedly sharing what you are going to do, you are internalizing the action point, and are becoming more accountable for it. The same principle applies here. The action points are refined and further developed during the group sharing sessions as well. People may offer support or knowledge from an unexpected source, and it is common for people to realize that their action points overlap with those of another person, creating an ally.

It is possible for everyone to share their individual action points together in a large group, skipping the small group sharing, but this is unadvised. Groups of three are much less intimidating than having to share in front of a larger group. Also, people gain clarity during each round of group sharing, which makes for sharp, clear, focused actions when the sharing is done and it is time to place them on the roadmap.

1. Focus the group on solutions that need actioning.
2. In order to ensure that participants will take responsibility, start with individual actions: "what am I going to do ?"
3. Let participants discuss and refine their action points as much as possible in changing small groups (Steal with Pride!).
4. Visualize actions; What, Who, When
5. Ask the group to evaluate whether all solutions have adequate action points; add and delete actions.

Figure 37: Actioning with Idealogue.

I mentioned earlier that the roadmap appeals to those who need clarity and something concrete. Idealogue is needed for those who love to talk. Combining the sharing in small groups with the actioning tool of road mapping appeals to both types of people, which is why the combination is so well received and so effective.

Chapter 9

Planning a Workshop

I have taught facilitation to thousands of students. Before beginning their training, most of my students already know a group tool or two, but they typically do not know how to properly plan a workshop with the tools they know. If you do not know how to plan a workshop, you can hardly bring concrete results with the tools - no matter how fantastic they are. My greatest gift to my students has been a clear framework on how to structure a workshop and in this chapter I will try to give you this framework and to explain how Idealogue can be used as one of the workshop tools.

So far we have seen chapter by chapter how Idealogue can be used effectively in different contexts; visioning, problem solving, deployment of ideas, creativity sessions, and actioning. These individual contexts are actually the building blocks of a workshop. To be clear, a workshop is not necessarily some special three-day event where the whole company goes camping together in the woods, although it could be. When I use the term *workshop*, all I am referring to is a meeting where people talk extensively about a specific topic, and work together to make progress regarding that topic. A workshop can be all about solving a specific problem, creatively thinking of new ideas, implementing a new strategy, or something else entirely. One difference between workshops and typical meetings is that workshops are much more interactive, and require people to work together and participate in group level activities.

Convergent and Divergent Thinking: An Important Balance

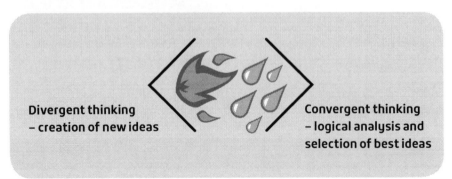

Divergent thinking – creation of new ideas

Convergent thinking – logical analysis and selection of best ideas

Figure 38: Two types of thinking that need to be accounted for when planning a workshop.

The key building block of a workshop is divergent and convergent thinking. A brilliant psychologist named J.P. Guilford helps us better understand the content of the workshop stages with two terms he introduced, *convergent thinking* and *divergent thinking*[8]. Guilford says that *divergent thinking* is when new ideas are created. *Divergent thinking* is often thought of as thinking creatively. *Convergent thinking* is basically the opposite and is thought of as thinking logically. Instead of seeking open ended or abstract answers, *convergent thinking* is looking for the right answer. Each stage of a workshop should blend divergence and convergence, and helping people come up with and choose ideas is what facilitation tools do. But each tool does it differently.

---

[8] Guilford first introduced these terms in his book, *The Nature of Human Intelligence*, which was published in 1967 by McGraw-Hill, of New York.

Typical Divergence and Convergence: Participants spend a long time creating ideas and a very short time choosing them

Divergence and Convergence with Idealogue: Participants spend a short time creating lots of ideas and a long time creating understanding and choosing ideas

Figure 39: The difference between divergence and convergence with and without Idealogue.

A balance between divergent and convergent thinking is needed to allow people to perform at high levels and succeed in reaching the goals of a workshop. A lot of times a workshop uses tools that emphasize *divergent thinking,* while *convergent thinking* is neglected or done very quickly in the end. This results in a lot of good ideas, but little to no group level understanding or internalization of these ideas. Actually the participants typically leave a little confused without understanding what happened and they might say, "It was a fun workshop, we created lots of ideas and we prioritized and decided on something... but I do not remember what it was." Idealogue attempts to correct the common imbalance between *divergent and convergent thinking.* With Idealogue, people only spend a brief amount of time thinking of ideas during the individual stage at the beginning, and a significant amount of time in groups sharing and stealing the ideas of others, developing and actually choosing the best ideas. This results in fewer ideas, but better ideas and better understanding of ideas.

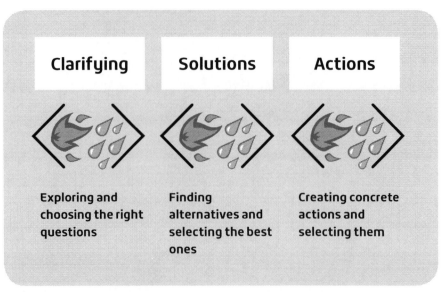

Clarifying	Solutions	Actions
Exploring and choosing the right questions	Finding alternatives and selecting the best ones	Creating concrete actions and selecting them

Figure 40: The three stages of a workshop.

When planning a workshop it is essential to know that workshops follow a predictable structure involving three stages; *clarifying*, *solutions* and *action*. Each stage is divergent and convergent in nature. This structure is called the C-S-A framework for short.

The Clarifying Stage

A workshop begins with the *clarifying* stage where the topic of the workshop is refined by the group. This stage clearly defines the subject matter, and also this stage ensures that everyone has a common understanding of the issue. Doing this allows for people to be more in synch and have more common ground when working together on solutions and needed actions in the later stages of a workshop. In the *clarifying* stage Idealogue is used, along with other facilitative tools.

Before the *clarifying* stage begins, you need to identify your objective. There are a few different possibilities:

1. If you are seeking long term development or a new idea is the topic, you should be clarifying a goal or a vision (Chapter 4: Visioning).
2. If there is a problem, conflict, or urgent issue, then you should be clarifying the problem (Chapter 5: Problem Solving).
3. If the goal has already been chosen, you should clarify understanding of that goal (Chapter 6: Deployment Meeting).

The Solutions Stage

The second stage of a workshop is the *solutions* stage. In this stage ideas and alternatives are thought of, with the best ones then being selected. Remember the example of our friend Peter Smudge struggling with creativity in Chapter seven? That example was the *solutions* stage of an innovation workshop. Usually Idealogue is not used during the *solutions* stage of a workshop, but in the example of Peter and DGD, it was a good choice because they were attempting to find solutions for one singular question as opposed to different distinct questions.

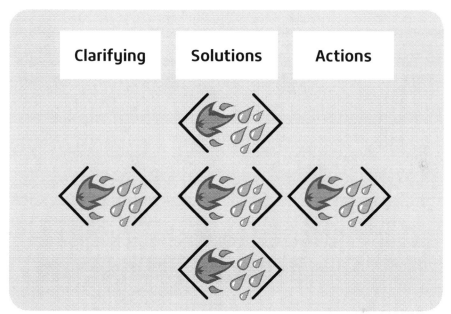

Figure 41: The solutions stage of a workshop deals with multiple questions, which makes it unsuitable for Idealogue.

To best explain why Idealogue isn't always suitable for solution stage, let's go back to the *clarifying* stage once again, using the example of Soundless Components and their production problem from Chapter 5.

The session starts with everyone thinking of reasons why the production problem is occurring. Over the course of the session, different ideas are thought of, shared and stolen, and then agreed upon. The Soundless components employees thought the problem was due to a lack of innovation and underpaid and underappreciated production workers. These two causes are the result of the problem solving session. But what next? The problem solving session ends, and the group then begins the *solutions* stage with two questions;

1. What are the solutions to the lack of innovation?
2. What are the solutions to underpaid and underappreciated production workers?

With Idealogue you cannot really think of two questions simultaneously because you cannot concentrate enough on either topic. And with this case we are very lucky that the group found only two problems. Typically you find many problems. And this is not only related to problems. *Clarifying* stages typically end with multiple questions. When you have a visioning session you end up with multiple goals or vision elements and when you deploy goals you typically want to deploy many different goals. In these cases, instead of Idealogue, a workshop tool designed for multiple questions would be a better choice. Solid alternatives to Idealogue when there are multiple questions or focuses in play are the Café and Open Space Technology, and I want to take a moment to explain them both.

The Café and Open Space: Additional Tools for Solution Stage

The Café Method has many names; Learning Café, Group Expo, Poster method, and finally its most recognizable name, the World Café. The method is often called café because it recreates the atmosphere found in coffee shops around the world; small tables of four to five people lost in conversation. This method also is often used with small groups working around flip-chart easels. Café methods are similar to Idealogue in the sense that people are working in small groups that repeatedly change, but there are also several key differences.

As people rotate from table to table in café method, one person stays behind and explains their topic to the new group members, and discussion ensues. Due to the person staying behind and explaining, the café method covers multiple topics at once.

1. Choosing topics
   – typically you have 3-4 questions selected during the clarifying stage
2. Group work
   – divide people into groups of equal size- each group writes down ideas and suggestions on the flipchart
3. Rotation
   – one member stays to tell the next participants what was discussed / everyone moves between groups- new groups produce more ideas / comment on the suggestions of previous groups
4. Conclusion
   – choose the best ideas and present - evaluation of ideas

Figure 42: Stages of the Café method. The café is a great tool for sharing ideas in situations when multiple questions are being asked.

The Café method strives to create a relaxed atmosphere of listening to others and acquiring information. The relaxed atmosphere of the Café method is very different than the competitive nature of the central rule of Idealogue, *steal with pride*.

Remember the sessions I had in Lagos with Assorted Nigeria Limited? After the *clarifying* stage where the participants thought of the ideal vision for the future I would then use the Café method with that group during the *solutions* stage. The café method is a good choice because questions relating to the new company vision for Assorted Nigeria Limited are equally important to all participants. Everyone is working towards a common company vision, and since all of the employees come from a similar working background, there are not technical questions that would pertain to some people, while being irrelevant to others.

The café method works best when the multiple questions are common for all participants. Typical examples of common questions are team development issues, values and a new strategy or vision. It is important to know that when new strategies are being discussed, the café method can work with multiple questions, but it is best for each table to focus on one question at a time, and then the facilitator can instruct the group to change topics.

If the contexts or questions during the *solutions* stage are understood only by experts and do not necessarily need commitment from everyone, then the right tool to use is Open Space or one of its simple variations. Open Space is basically a free form meeting. Each context or question is given its own space in the room and people naturally gravitate to what interests them, flowing from one topic to the next as they please.

- Meetings with no fixed agenda or premeditated structure.
- Developed by Harrison Owen in the 1980's and outlined in his book, "Open Space Technology: A User's Guide".
- These types of meetings have been used extensively in all types of business situations and also in community events.
- The meeting format works for groups that range from just a few people up to thousands of people.
- For more information on Open Space Technology (OST), check out the links below:
- www.openspaceworld.com
- http://www.peace.ca/ost.htm
- Owen, Harrison. Open Space Technology: A User's Guide. San Francisco: Berrett-Koehler Publishers, 1997.

Figure 43: Open Space Technology.

Between these context-specific sub-meetings, people float as they please, contributing what they can. Open Space meetings are very simple to organize and run, and are good for groups ranging from just a few people to hundreds.

1. Choose topics with the group during the clarifying stage
2. Re-introduce the topics. There can be several simultaneous topics (3-10 depending on the size of the group)
3. Introduce the roles
   The meeting leader is responsible for holding the meeting, making sure that the meeting is documented and also prioritizing key solutions with the group. Participants pool their skills for use by the meeting leaders (if they can contribute to several meetings, they go from one meeting to another). During the course of the meeting, people can choose to go to whatever meeting they like (this freedom of choice is called the Law of two feet).
4. Connect topics with meeting leaders by:
   - Assigning topics
     or
   - Asking for volunteers
5. Give each topic a meeting place
6. Tell the group how much time they have and let them begin
7. After the time is up, have the meeting leaders present the content of their meeting to the entire group

Make sure to give enough time to the group so people can visit several meetings.

Figure 44: A simple variation of Open Space and its steps for the solutions stage.

Idealogue simply does not work when you have many simultaneous questions, which there usually are during the *solutions* stage. Idealogue is based around the individual instruction of "steal with pride and collect the best ideas on your own sheet of paper." For this to work, the topic has to be a single prompt, issue, goal, or question. If you are working simultaneously with many questions it just becomes a mess. In these cases you need to replace Idealogue with a different tool.

Converging with Idealogue

What is this nonsense?! Supposedly this is a book about Idealogue and all of a sudden Pepe writes that the method is not suitable in some situations, and now other methods are introduced. Where is Idealogue now? Do not worry; these other methods which are designed for multiple topics or questions need help. They do not work well alone, and they are much more effective when they are combined with Idealogue.

According to the philosophy of Open Space Technology, everyone does not need to understand or participate in all decisions. Open Space is a large group method created for dealing with complexity, and in complex situations it is just not possible for every single person to be involved in all of the decision making processes.

How about if you are working in a team and decisions are highly interdependent? Everyone should at least understand the logic of each other's decisions. This is where Open Space relies on self-organizing. With Open Space, participants freely connect and decide for themselves which questions are relevant and important to them, and team members and people with interdependent decisions usually end up self-organizing so that they are informed of the decisions of others that affect their own work.

Café methods are excellent in creating a good conversion around multiple topics and exploring options, but how about creating consensus and making decisions? When using Café methods facilitators rely on small groups or prioritizing to make decisions. We have a long fruitful talk to create options and then we choose ideas in few minutes. Once again we have an imbalance of divergence and convergence.

The methods for multiple questions worked well in creating options for many simultaneous questions. Now, to support convergence and consensus creation we recommend Idealogue. Now you have the groups finished their work with many simultaneous questions. You start Idealogue and everyone chooses the best solutions on their own piece of paper. Next you ask groups of three to steal ideas and you then form new small groups of three and repeat this step several times. When converging with Idealogue you will have the groups comparing different options and justifying their decisions. A further understanding is created and the group is again closer to consensus. Or, at the very least they understand each other's logic behind the decisions. After a couple of rounds of stealing you choose and post the best solutions. You may prioritize if it is still needed.

Action Stage

As we saw in chapter 8: Actioning, Idealogue is used once again at this stage to get people talking with one another to find unexpected sources of assistance and support. The Roadmap activity was also used so that a concrete reminder of the actions to be taken was created, and also to organize the multiple actions of the company into one place. Combining Idealogue with the Roadmap during the *action* stage is something I love to do because of its effectiveness, and you will notice this structure repeated in all sample workshop outlines shown in the end of this section.

Sample Workshops

Let's recapture the key principles and finally get into planning workshops. There are typically three stages in a workshop; clarifying, solutions, and the action stage. If you have more stages you are probably trying to do something too complicated and the participants will most likely struggle to keep up with your logic.

In the clarifying stage you have one question and you can always use Idealogue but there are three types of workshops; topics you are clarifying might require additional tools depending on whether you are clarifying a problem, vision or deploying a goal. I am going to explain the flow of each type here.

In the solutions stage Idealogue might not be useable if you are dealing with multiple questions. A better choice of a tool would be café method when you have questions that are important for all participants and a simple Open Space variation works better when you are dealing with expert questions.

In the action stage there is always one question: "What am I going to do?" and you may use Idealogue again.

If it is a problem that is being clarified, then you need a problem solving workshop. In figure 45, you can see a sample outline of a problem solving workshop that shows the entire CSA format, with root cause analysis and Idealogue used in the *clarifying* stage. For a problem solving workshop, an analytical problem solving tool like root cause analysis may be a good choice. An advantage of using root cause analysis at this stage is that everyone has had time to think of the logic behind the problem which makes the stealing of ideas and repeated small group work stages run smoothly: people have already thought about the problem, so their ideas and answers are more logical.

Open Space meetings are great for the *solution stage* of a problem solving workshop. Many times the solutions to problems which affect a group can be divided and technical, requiring insider knowledge and specialization. This is why Open Space is a good fit. People can gravitate towards the solutions which they understand and help contribute to those specific conversations with their expertise.

Like all workshops, the problem solving workshop ends with the *actions* stage. It is in this stage where the finer details are outlined and assigned. After completing this stage there should be clear 'who', 'what', and 'when' roles assigned.

1. **Clarifying; Defining the Problem**
   - Tool; Idealogue and Root-cause-analysis
2. **Solutions**
   - Tool; Open Space
3. **Actions**
   - Tool; Idealogue and Roadmap

Figure 45: A sample structure for problem solving workshop.

Sometimes important decisions or new strategies are developed by a small minority, and they affect a great majority. If a goal or vision is given from the top-down, for example from upper management to a larger group of employees, then you have a workshop to deploy that goal or vision. Workshops that deal in this type of context are called deployment workshops.

1. **Clarifying; The change goals**
   - **Presentation of the change and what it hopes to accomplish**
   - **Tools; Idealogue and two questions (key facts and first reaction)**
2. **Solutions**
   - **Tool; Café Method. Seeking solutions to achieve the goals of the change**
3. **Actions**
   - **Tools; Idealogue and Roadmap**

Figure 46: The framework of a deployment workshop.

Figure 46 shows the framework for a deployment workshop, and at first glance, it appears that it follows the normal CSA framework. It basically does, but the difference in deployment workshops is how Idealogue is used in the *clarifying* stage. Idealogue begins as normal with an individual stage, but in this stage people are asked to keep two questions in mind:

1. What were the key fact of the presentation?
2. What is my first reaction to this presentation?

During the solution stage of a deployment workshop you could use Idealogue if you had one goal to deploy; for instance company growth. Typically, companies have many goals that they need to deploy; for example a company may have annual goals to increase employee satisfaction by 5%, lower overall spending by 8%, and maintain a growth rate of 10%. Each employee should be committed and therefore participate in finding the best solutions for each goal. The Café method is a tool which can both handle multiple questions and create commitment, which makes it a good choice for the *solutions* stage of a deployment workshop. In the end of the workshop, the Roadmap tool and Idealogue are recommended.

1. **Clarifying; Vision**
   - **Tools; Idealogue and Wishing**
2. **Solutions**
   - **Tool; Café method**
3. **Action**
   - **Tool; Idealogue and Roadmap**

Figure 47: The "CSA" structure of a strategy workshop.

If we need a new direction for the company, then a strategy workshop would be appropriate. Take a moment to look at figure 47; the sample CSA structure of a strategy workshop[9]. We have the familiar *clarifying* stage which uses Idealogue, along with the wishing activity, which was to help give people freedom to think big and dream during the individual phase of Idealogue. In the *solutions* stage we use the Café method because everyone should understand the strategic solutions and the café method forces everyone to participate. Also be sure to take note of the *action* stage, which has the now familiar combination of Idealogue and the Roadmap activity.

The aim of this chapter was to help you plan workshops and to choose the right tools for different stages. If you are ever in doubt when choosing tools, refer back to the workshop frameworks shown in figures 45, 46, and 47, and remember that Idealogue is always a good idea in the opening and closing stages of a workshop.

---

[9] If you want to try a little more advanced version of a strategy workshop, you may ask participants to think of barriers to reaching the vision simultaneously with solutions. Exploring barriers will make participants think on a deeper level and therefore improve the solutions that are proposed during the session.

Conclusion

Current brainstorming techniques leave something to be desired, and often give poor results. Do you agree with that now that you have finished reading about Idealogue? To be honest, I don't really care what you think about traditional brainstorming methods. What I do hope for is that you have picked up some material that helps you plan and conduct future meetings and workshops better than before.

Idealogue is a powerful tool, and one that I believe in. It helps people share their ideas and it allows people to accept and adopt ideas coming from other people too, helping to develop a better understanding of people and their ideas and building consensus and commitment along the way.

I hope you try Idealogue in your own work, and please, STEAL IT WITH PRIDE!

Afterword

By Dr. Greg O' Shea

Global warming, globalization, and global ageing are some of the great challenges of this century. To continue to grow economically Europe must find ways to support and encourage better health amongst the aged and reduce the cost of maintaining older populations. Technology provides one answer but, drawing on the lessons of the past, it is imperative that these answers come 'bottom up', from entrepreneurs, from academics, from the public sector, and from consumers.

To do this it is essential that these groups of people connect together, on an equal footing, share their perceptions of problems and share their possible solutions in order to be able to plan the steps that they can take together to solve these problems. To achieve this, the barriers to true dialogue need to be addressed. Idealogue is a facilitation tool that seeks to address this critical issue.

Idealogue is inspired by notions of open innovation and how this can be done in practice – how do we drive intensive collaboration between different stakeholders to stimulate co-creation, to catalyze open innovation and encourage individuals and communities to drive bottom-up innovation initiatives to societal challenges. It provides a collaborative context and process that brings concrete outcomes and at the same time shapes a special quality of interaction. This is a deceptively simple tool that is important to the way we work together in the future.

Dr. Greg O' Shea is a facilitator and a co-creator of idealogue. He holds degrees in law, an MBA, and he also is a certified accountant and auditor. He currently holds a position on the faculty of both Aalto University and Anglia Ruskin University.

What's next?

You have just read about the different stages of a workshop. Now you can see them being used firsthand by attending an Idealogue training seminar. Become familiar with the tools and concepts discussed in this book by seeing them demonstrated and using them yourself in a training seminar that is personalized to your specific working environment and needs. Visit www.Idealoguemethod.com for more information.

To learning more facilitation tools please visit www.grapepeople.fi/en/.

I have two upcoming books that will be published within the next year; a handbook of Facilitation that focuses on the best facilitation tools and also a book on Facilitative Leadership and how it applies to practical, everyday working situations. Visit www.grapepeople.fi/en to keep an eye out for further announcements regarding these books, which will also be available to order from www.amazon.com.

Printed in Great Britain
by Amazon